Vocational success equals happiness.

The author equates the two—and why not? Why ignore the happiness potential, the pleasure possibility of this dimension of life, when so much of waking, active life is devoted to work! Most of us must work: some for physical survival, some for intellectual stimulation and growth, others for the human companionship nurtured by a healthy work environment.

To attain vocational success and its complement, happiness, use the Luntz astrological guidance techniques. Then choose the career most compatible with your personal desires, inner motivations, and natural talents.

All you need is a working knowledge of astrology; Mr. Luntz furnishes the astrological tools and rules for exploring all aspects of vocational choice.

- how to select an occupation appropriate to your individual needs and desires
- how to determine the most favorable time to start a new enterprise
- when to apply for a new position
- how to select a business partner
- how to approach—understand—employer-employee relationships

Frustrated by a job that stifles your personality and ignores your natural aptitudes? You can realize vocational success, career satisfaction, happiness and personal fulfillment: Mr. Luntz shows you how to use your personal astrological pattern for success *and* happiness.

You *can* have both!

VOCATIONAL GUIDANCE
BY
ASTROLOGY

A LLEWELLYN ASTROLOGICAL MANUAL

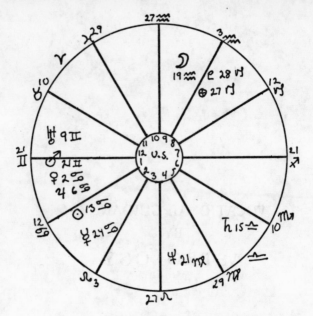

THE UNITED STATES OF AMERICA

Nations have horoscopes based on the day, hour and minute of their first existence, just as individuals. Every organization, in fact, every group, even every undertaking has its own birth moment. The U.S. natal chart is on authority of the very great astrologer, Alan Leo, who offers two, with this one preferred. The writer has used it in public forecasts since 1938, and it has in virtually every case proved authentic and enabled a correct prediction to be made of the outcome of a national or international situation.

We are a Gemini people, dexterous, intelligent, manually skilful and not too orderly in some things, with the emotional characteristics of our Cancer Sun. The United States has by far the best natal chart of any great nation—26 good aspects to 10 adverse—with England running it a close second. In leadership its five planets including the Sun, fully justify the role it has assumed in the world; in patience and determination its Fixed signs are completely adequate, yet there are enough Common signs to make our people as a whole flexible in ideas and appreciative of other nations and their cultures.

From our chart as compared with the nativities of other countries, it seems that no nation can ultimately prevail against the United States, though our one really bad planet, Neptune, has caused us a lot of trouble.

It is said that Benjamin Franklin was responsible for bringing this country into being during the night of July 4th, 1776, when Congress spent hours debating whether or not The Declaration of Independence should be signed. When the decision was unanimous, the United States was born. Ben did a first rate job, eliminating almost every bad aspect, but alas, he had never heard of Neptune and Pluto, though Uranus had just been discovered and its two influences in our chart are trines—wholly favorable.

Neptune ruling subversion, with its two exact squares to the Ascendant, and in its detriment (the only badly placed planet we have), is our sole major threat, but with a natal chart showing 72% of good aspects against 28% adverse, and with 50% of our planets and angles in mental signs (the average is 25%), we are likely to continue as world leaders and even world thinkers for an indefinite time to come.

VOCATIONAL
GUIDANCE BY
ASTROLOGY

Charles E. Luntz

1962
LLEWELLYN PUBLICATIONS
P.O. Box 3383, St. Paul, Minn. 55165, U.S.A.

ISBN 0-87542-448-1 (cloth)
ISBN 0-87542-435-X (paper)

Revised Edition 1962
Reprinted 1969
Reprinted 1971
Reprinted 1973

Publisher: Llewellyn Publications, St. Paul, MN
Typographers: Twin City Graphic Photon Inc.; Chester-Kent, Inc.
Lithographer: R. R. Donnelley & Sons Co., Chicago, IL

Printed in the United States of America

TO MY WIFE

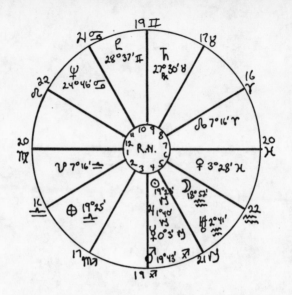

RICHARD NIXON
PRESIDENT OF THE UNITED STATES

One of the most remarkable comebacks in modern political history must be credited to President Nixon who, a few years before his election to the presidency, was virtually washed out by the press, radio and TV commentators as a "has-been." And at the time Mr. Nixon himself seems to have shared that view.

Attention should be directed to the very full fourth house (outcomes), containing the Sun, his ruler Mercury, Jupiter and Mars. Between them they have six favorable aspects to five unfavorable, but to these may be added Neptune in Cancer (two to one good), normal fourth house sign, and the Moon, ruler of Cancer, (two good, one adverse)—and the Moon has an exact trine to Nixon's MidHeaven which would for him govern the presidency, the highest station to which he could aspire.

This ten to seven advantage in the factors governing outcomes is a very good example of the way in which influences "break" in a natal chart. The seven adverse aspects most certainly did their nefarious work in bygone years when his political lot consisted largely of frustrations and disappointments, but he came back magnificently by aid of his beneficent "outcome" influences, to the wonderment of those who had dismissed him as completely eliminated him from the presidential picture.

Mr. Nixon has a powerful and well balanced horoscope. Combination of the highly intelligent Virgo, one of its best degrees rising, with the tenacious Capricorn, and plus the Moon and the Saturnine co-ruler also Uranus in Fixed signs, indicate a native who does not know how to quit. His four planets in Cardinal signs, including as a planet the Sun, his ruler Mercury, Jupiter and Neptune, bestow fine leadership ability, while three planets and all four angles in Common signs, tone down the asperity of Capricorn, giving him a likeable personality, reasonable and able to comprehend points of view in opposition to his own. The benefic Dragon's Head in the seventh house (public enemies) would confirm this.

As with most practical politicians or statesmen, the Earthy (practical) signs are very full, containing the Sun, Mercury, Saturn and the Ascendant. The President can face facts, profit by experience, and is undoubtedly very competent in the things he does. He should make a very good First Executive—perhaps one of the best.

PREFACE

In no field is the usefulness of astrology more demonstrable than in that of vocational guidance. Yet hardly any branch of the mighty science of the stars has been more neglected. With a few exceptions it has been relegated to a chapter or two in general works on astrology or is scattered promiscuously through interpretative material dealing with the signs, planets and houses.

Here and there a writer has essayed to produce a specialized work on "Vocational Astrology" and has contributed interesting and valuable additions to the general knowledge. The present volume, however, aims at a much more exhaustive exposition than seems yet to have been attempted. While it presumes some elementary acquaintance with the subject, including the ability to cast and progress a horoscope, or at least to examine understandingly one cast and progressed by someone else, it takes nothing for granted otherwise.

Appendices at the end of the book will enable the beginner to interpret the symbols used and to know what works he may obtain to familiarize himself with the rudiments of astrology. Certain other explanatory material is provided in Appendix B, for purposes of clarification.

The rules or laws which must guide the judgment in determining the most suitable vocation are stated simply but with the utmost wealth of detail. The reader should have little difficulty in applying them to his own or any horoscope. This book, however, is also intended as a comprehensive reference work for those in professional practice. The day of the Vocational Astrologer is only now dawning. Other systems for determining the natural aptitudes of young people, valuable enough in their respective ways, can at best be only partial guides. The natal horoscope, properly interpreted, leaves nothing to chance—sees all, knows all, tells all.

No service to the community can be greater than one which will effectually place each of its members in the exact niche where each belongs. The purpose of this work is to show how to accomplish this supremely important end. It is not too much to say that if such an aim could be universally achieved a large number of our economic difficulties, due to the wretched misplacement in industrial and professional life of millions of our people, would automatically disappear.

PREFACE TO SECOND EDITION

VOCATIONAL GUIDANCE BY ASTROLOGY made its debut just 20 years ago and apparently filled a long felt need as it has been out of print for many years. A constant succession of orders for the book both from the public and from the trade have continued to come in and as the original publishers had merged with a British firm in the meantime, no reprint was feasible.

The present publishers commissioned the author to revise the work, bringing it up to date in the light of researches and discoveries in the astrological field during the past two decades. This has been done and a chapter added on the vocational influence of Pluto, the most recently discovered planet, also three additional horoscopes and their elucidations — Khrushchev's, Lyndon Johnson's and Nelson Rockefeller's.

Forecasts made in the 1942 edition which have since come to pass are indicated by asterisks and a footnote. They are valuable as evidence that the horoscope, properly interpreted, is in very fact a guide to the trend of one's destiny. It does not, however, "tell fortunes." The natal chart assuredly shows in what fields the greatest possibility of good fortune resides. It does not insure that the native (subject of the horoscope) will cultivate these fields or go anywhere near them. He has free will. He can do exactly the things the horoscope indicates are disadvantageous for him. Or he can follow this God-given guide to success and well-being.

But he must do his part. The horoscope will point the

way but it will not do the work for him. As an example, a native might possess an excellent fifth house (a department of the horoscope), showing good influences for investments such as stocks and bonds. At a certain period these influences might be stirred into action. If he used ordinary prudence in making his selections during this period taking into account the factors any careful investor would consider and not buying blindly, his chances of profit would be good. But if he did all these things when his current influences on investments were adverse, he would still be likely to lose or at least wind up with a profitless transaction.

This is neither theory nor imagination but is based on the author's lengthy experience, both in making his own investments and advising others. Similarly, while a good tenth house and its affiliates (Saturn and Capricorn) show high possibilities of business or professional success, this will not come without the personal efforts of the native, nor without proper training for the type of occupation the horoscope shows he is qualified to engage in.

Here again, the training should begin at the right astrological time (for him — it might be the wrong time for someone else). Always it is the individual's own horoscope that must be the guide, not the day-by-day aspects of the Sun, Moon and planets to each other. These, when favorable do help somewhat, and when unfavorable mitigate a little against the horoscopic influences. But the horoscope is a personal not a generalized thing and must be so treated.

If the present work is employed with these fundamentals borne in mind, it should be of the utmost help in choosing a suitable career and in timing the steps to be taken to implement it.

CONTENTS

Contents

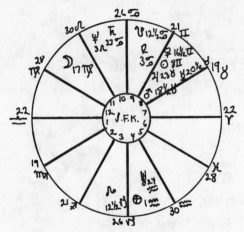

JOHN F. KENNEDY
FORMER UNITED STATES PRESIDENT

If ever a tragic end to a distinguished career was written in the heavens, assuredly the natal chart of the murdered President portrays this one in all its ghastly detail.

President Kennedy was assassinated while riding in an automobile in Dallas, a far way from his birthplace in Massachusetts, in a southwesterly direction. The eighth house rules death; Mars, particularly in its detriment as it is here, governs violent death including an end to the life by shooting, Venus and Jupiter in the house a comparatively painless transition, the Sun a death accompanied by much post-mortem fame or publicity.

Four planets and the Sun are in Kennedy's lethal house. Mars (shooting) and Mercury (transportation) exactly on the cusp of the house, its strongest position. Pluto, death planet, is in the ninth house, the southwest angle of his chart. The malefic Dragon's Tail is also in the ninth. And the malignant Saturn is in the same position on top of the MidHeaven, as in the charts of both Napoleon and Hitler, though the latter's Saturn was 9 degrees away from the exact MidHeaven degree and he maintained his leadership longer.

Kennedy was astrologically warned not to go to Dallas at that particular time in 1963 but, as reported over TV, he replied that he would rather trust in God than in astrology. The present writer, who was on several radio and TV programs, both before and after the tragic event, took leave to inquire who Mr. Kennedy thought had created the stars and planets and ordained "Let them be for signs" (Genesis I:14), if not God.

Did this promising young life have to terminate at age 46 in such grievous fashion?

No informed astrologer could doubt, after examining the grim eighth house, the unaspected Pluto, which without aspects is highly malefic, and the other significant factors above cited, that his violent death was indicated as at least possible if not probable. And yet it would seem not to have been completely inevitable. While Uranus afflicting three of the planets in the house had good aspects which might have averted it had Mr. Kennedy heeded the sound astrological advice given him.

Would it have come later in any case? Perhaps—but had he known the significance of his own horoscope and guided himself by proper precautionary measures, perhaps not.

But what *did* happen is shown in such crystal clear fashion that of itself it answers every objection to the validity of astrology that those unschooled in the science can advance.

VOCATIONAL GUIDANCE
BY
ASTROLOGY

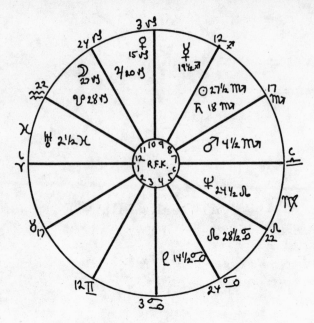

ROBERT F. KENNEDY
FORMER U.S. ATTORNEY GENERAL

There are extraordinary analogies between the horoscopes of the two murdered brothers. Whereas John had the lesser malefic Mars exactly on the cusp of the lethal eighth house, Saturn, the great malefic is in precisely the same position. Robert's eighth house cusp is in 17 degrees Scorpio (the death sign), John's is in 19 degrees Taurus, virtually opposite. Both had the Sun in the eighth.

The former President had every planet but one above the earth, signifying success early in life. This brother had every planet but two above the earth. Both achieved the same post-mortem celebrity indicated by the eighth house Sun.

Robert's natal chart was by far the stronger of the two, with its powerful Aries-Scorpio complex, but both charts were those of very able personages—John with 27 good to 17 adverse aspects, and Robert 31 good, 15 adverse. Of the two it would seem that the former possessed the greater charm in spite of the constant endowing of Robert by the publicity media with super-charissma. Aries-Scorpio is astrologically noted for a number of fine characteristics when the horoscope is good, but charm is hardly one of them.

The brothers, like most people in political life, had their foes, and both had Mars in the seventh house (public enemies). All of these family resemblances in their charts can hardly be dismissed as coincidences, especially as they were born eight years apart in different months and at different birth times.

The influence on both natives of the father is strongly indicated by Saturn (male parent) with four favorable aspects to one unfavorable in John's chart—five to one in Robert's, although Saturn's unhappy position in the latter's horoscope squaring Neptune ultimately did its violent work.

Could Robert have made the presidency had he lived? The answer can only be speculative as he didn't live to attain it, but with both benefics in the tenth house, a splendidly aspected Saturn ruling Capricorn on the MidHeaven, it is somewhat more than probable that he could.

CHAPTER I

Its Need

ONE of the weakest features of our civilization is the haphazard fashion in which our young people are permitted to select what they hope will be their life's work. Worse still, it may be selected for them, in which case the chance that the ideal choice may be made is even more remote. The schools and colleges, the instructors, the parents, the youngsters themselves, do their best to make a wise selection. Sometimes they succeed. Far more often they miserably fail.

It is comparatively rare to meet a man (or woman) who is perfectly happy in his chosen vocation. The test comes ten, twenty, thirty years later, perhaps. If he is one of the multitude of parents who declare, "I don't want my son to follow my profession," it may be taken for granted even though he may deny it, that in some manner or other that profession is uncongenial to him. This may bring a challenge from the successful. "I am a doctor," a physician may say. "I have made a satisfactory competence. I have achieved some recognition in my field. I enjoy my work. But I don't want my son to follow in my footsteps. My time is never my own. The hours are completely irregular. I may have to turn out in the middle of the night after an exhausting day and drive five miles because Mrs. Brown's baby has colic. Half the time I don't get paid." And so on and on—all perfectly true. Let Junior get into something easier. But the doctor who talks like that is obviously far from satisfied with his own profession even though he has contrived to be reasonably successful in it. If he were satisfied, there is no other profession in which he would desire his son to be, unless, of course, the latter had obvious talents in another direction or none at all in this. And even then his father would see with lingering regret the boy preparing to follow some alien line of endeavor.

Because the man who is wholly and completely successful in his work is the man to whom no other vocation appears possible. He is so wrapped up in it—he loves it so unreservedly—that it would seem a sort of blasphemy to him to stress its inconveniences and use them as an excuse for his son to pass it by. If he were a medical man, he might tell the youth, "Yes, the hours are long and irregular, you work like a dog and when you think you are done for the night you may have to start all over again. Your patients often may not pay you. All these things and many more you will have to contend with. But," he would conclude in a tremendous burst of enthusiasm, "it's the only profession in the world, my boy, and those things are trifling inconveniences that don't matter. I can't imagine myself in anything else. And I shall be the happiest man alive if you decide to follow in my footsteps."

There speaks the truly successful man, and if his horoscope were expertly examined it would be found that as a physician he was "a natural." He would be the "one in a thousand" who somehow had contrived to discover his niche and to fill it. To him his profession is his life and he glories in it. And for doctor one may substitute lawyer, business man, engineer, artist, writer, politician, teacher, contractor, scientist, social service worker or any other of a hundred or a thousand vocations open to civilized man.

What makes the "successful man," and what accounts for the myriads of failures?

Disregarding the conclusions of the vocational specialists, some of which undoubtedly have merit, we return the unequivocal answer, which does not necessarily conflict with these conclusions, that success is found where the obvious trends of the natal horoscope have been followed; failure, where they have been disregarded.

We must, of course, avoid over-simplification of the problem. A man of strong will-power, fixed determination and perseverance, may achieve moderate success in a vocation for which his horoscope shows him to be unfitted. But the horoscope also shows the preponderance of fixed signs and other indicators that mark the will that did it. To what heights, however, might this will not have carried him had he followed the lines of his natural aptitude as laid down in the natal chart? Swimming against the current is good exercise but slow progress. Enough natural obstacles are usually provided to the attainment of success that we need not go out of our way to seek artificial ones.

Here it may be pointed out that if the popular conception that man's future is cut and dried by his horoscope were true, vocational guidance by astrology would be impossible. But planetary and sidereal "influences," so called, merely chart the course. They do not force anyone to follow it. They declare in language plain to the astrologer, what any given person *should* do, for greatest success and happiness. They by no means proclaim that he *will* do it. He may choose just the opposite course. Fatalistic astrology, with all its will-weakening implications, disputes this but has never successfully disproved it. Man does have free will. The horoscope may urge—and for our own benefit. It does not dictate.

And a natural aptitude is also an urge. An Edison *must* invent. A Ford must manufacture. A George Bernard Shaw must write. A Kreisler must play. Can anyone imagine those named following vocations other than the ones in which they have reached such eminence? Their horoscopes indicate the measure of success each has attained and the lines along which each has marched to his goal. In each horoscope doubtless are to be found warning signs barring the way to success in many other fields which these men, so fortunate in their own, might have followed. Some of them, perhaps, they did follow for a time—finding themselves in blind alleys from which happily they were able to retreat. The life of almost every famous man contains early episodes of disappointment and failure due to wrong choice of a life-work. Sometimes it is, or seems to be, a forced choice. Inwardly the deep-seated urge is present to do something, anything, rather than the unpalatable drudgery which circumstances seem to have compelled. Somehow opportunity presents itself, is seized, made fullest use of, and the "lucky" man finds himself doing the one great thing he loves and is best fitted for.

But how many "career" tales have this happy ending? Statistics tell us the sad story of the few, the infinitesimally few, who reach the top "where there is always room." They tell us of the few more who wind up somewhere near the top, and of the small percentage of near-successes who land within range of the upper brackets. Immediately below them come a sprinkling of the good second-raters, then more, many more, third-raters, and we need not trouble to classify the fourth to the forty-sixth raters who constitute the rest of the population. They are the millions who go through life thwarted. Either they "haven't quite made it," or they have not come within a thousand miles of making it. They may be comfortably off or in poverty; well-known in their circle or obscure. That has little to do with it. Success may sometimes be a matter of money—and sometimes it may not be. Success may sometimes mean the limelight—and sometimes it may mean the cloister. These things are not its gauge or measure. True success is synonymous with happiness. Are you happy? Have you no regrets? Can you look about you in your work and say, "I can want nothing better at which to labor than this," and mean it? Has it given you, whether your income be large or small, enough to satisfy your tastes and those of your family, to provide for your future and theirs, and to gratify your desire (if it may be thus crudely expressed) to "amount to something"?

If you can answer all these questions with a quick affirmative, you are one of the few successes and we need not tell you you should be happy. You are happy.

But if the very questions bring a hollow laugh—if you have to answer no to all of them or to any of them, then in some particular you have fallen short. If you are too young to have reached the consummation stage—

if you are still struggling, still trying to find yourself, then does it seem you are on the way to an affirmative answer to all these questions? Young or old, if you are in the right line of work, you should be happy in it and have no regrets because you are not engaged in something else. And if you are still in the sacrifice-making stage which nearly all have to go through on their way up, they should be happy sacrifices, sacrifices you are glad to make because you can see forward in your mind's eye to a day when they will no longer be necessary. Meantime you are in your beloved work, whatever it may be, and the temporary self-denials are part of a price you do not begrudge paying because it is part of what goes with the job.

To those, and unfortunately their name is legion, whose work is hateful monotony, who look at it as something to keep body and soul together and nothing besides, it may seem incredible that one may regard labor in that light. Yet in the natal horoscope of each there is indicated just that kind of vocation for him. There is something he (or she) can do which will not seem like work but like play, so absolutely fitted is he to do that particular thing to perfection. And the tragedy is that most of these unsuccessful, resentful, baffled millions will (until selecting vocations by the horoscope is the law of the land) go through their entire lives without finding themselves.

Round pegs in square holes—square pegs in round holes; physicians who should have been lawyers and lawyers who should be designing houses, and failures in business who never should have entered business but who belong in one of the professions! The stupendous need for some absolutely certain way of determining natural aptitudes and linking up those aptitudes with their money-making possibilities (for man must live) surely need not be stressed.

It is of little use to ask the child, before his training begins, what he would like to be. He knows less about it than his parents and they probably know nothing. His answers may range from a street-car conductor to a fireman—or maybe he would like to be the man who reads the electric meter. It is hazardous to assume, because he "likes to draw," that he has the makings of an artist or architect. Nearly all children like to draw. It may be meaningful or entirely meaningless. He may play with soldiers a great deal, too, yet grow up to be a pacifist. His natural inclinations may have no opportunity to show themselves. Mozart might never have been a musician if his parents had been too poor to buy a piano or its Eighteenth Century forerunner, the harpsichord.

True, genius plus will surmounts the most staggering obstacles to manifest itself, but this work is not written wholly for geniuses. In every normal human being (and most of us are normal at base) there exists the capacity for doing some one thing (occasionally more than one) better than most of the others in our circle can do it. We can shine somewhere—excel in something or other. School and college may or may not bring it out. We may get switched onto another track—a false track—and waste years or a lifetime imagining we are good at something in which we are only mediocre. Opportunity may arise for us to swing into the very thing the horoscope cries out that we were meant to do. If the natal chart indicators are at all strong the opportunity is almost certain to arise. We may miss it entirely for want of recognition. We may be urged, begged, to make a change which would start us on the highroad to the success we crave. Yet doubt, fear, disinclination to make a move may keep us chained to a profession or business for which the horoscope shows we have poor aptitude and no likelihood of anything above mediocre returns.

There is, of course, another side to the question: the possibility of our being attracted to a vocation which will provide much inner satisfaction but meagre financial recompense. The horoscope shows that, too. Then it is up to us to make the choice. To some, monetary returns are a matter of indifference if they are in the work they love. Good and well, but isn't it wise to know ahead of time that the compensation is likely to be wholly spiritual? And there may be and probably is something else in the horoscope which will supply both.

Conversely, the natal chart may offer highly lucrative possibilities along lines in which the inner satisfactions will be nil. If the subject of the horoscope, or "native" as astrologers term him, regards the financial factor as all-important, he may select this rather than a "second-choice" which might be full of interest but from which the pecuniary gain would be less. That, too, is strictly up to him. It is not the province of this work to preach to anybody what they should or should not do, so far as their freedom of choice is concerned. The astrological facts will be presented, the astrological consequences of this, that, or the other course pointed out. The native may apply them as he will, to his own case.

This introductory chapter set out to show that a

need existed for some trustworthy guide to the selection of a life-work. It has attempted to show that conventional methods, valuable though they may be, are at best "hit-or-miss." It is more than probable that the really shrewd appraisers of human aptitudes are those who, while perhaps crediting their success to other methods, secretly rely on astrology. It is pretty well conceded that it is used extensively in Hollywood in casting important parts. The writer, who for 20 years has hired and trained a sales personnel of many hundreds, has, for more than half the time, relied on the aid furnished by a knowledge of astrology.

To the unfortunate folk who, not having the slightest familiarity with the subject, insist that it is all imagination, all he can say is that, if this be so, it seems to work just as well as the real thing. But it is not imagination. Astrology is one of the grandest and most perfect of sciences. In the forthcoming chapters its enormous possibilities as an aid to choosing the right vocation will be clearly set forth.

CHAPTER II

Its Principles

THE basic principles of vocational astrology, like those of astrology as a whole, are simple. Their ramifications, however, may become exceedingly complex. Yet when understood they are not unduly hard to apply to individual cases. It cannot be too often stressed, however, that *all*—not some but *all*—of the numerous factors in the natal chart must each be carefully studied, or correct judgment is impossible.

Right there is the weakness of the cheap vocational analysis cheerfully offered by incompetents, who haphazardly glance at two or three of these many configurations and positions (if they do that much) and then presume to pass on the business or professional talents of the native. It cannot be done that way with any hope of success. Nature has not made the natal horoscope too easy to read. She requires, in this branch of research as in all others, painstaking digging out of the facts—and then the exercise of careful thought and judgment as to what those facts mean.

Fortunately the modern astrologer falls heir to the vast body of knowledge accumulated over centuries and millennia which is embraced in the so-called traditional astrology. And in the main this traditional astrology is very sound. Some fanciful accretions doubtless have fastened themselves on the proven teachings as they came down the years. Sometimes these were the product of sensationalists eager for self-advertising by propounding something new, regardless of its truth. Occasionally they may be traced to sincere masters of the science working with insufficient knowledge. Thus Kepler, a very great astrologer, invented the minor aspects (in which this writer has not the slightest belief) to account for phenomena he could not otherwise explain. Kepler did not know of the existence of Uranus, Neptune or Pluto. He was handicapped by trying to account for conditions which in all probability the presence of these planets would amply explain. He formulated the so-called minor aspects, and there are enough of these constantly available to "explain" virtually anything.

Kepler meant well, but his "minor aspects" clutter up the horoscope with misleading junk which is not only valueless (at least in the writer's opinion) but positively harmful. Students who have always regarded these aspects as sacrosanct because they appear in well-known ephemerides and aspectarians, may be shocked by this conclusion, but they may be assured it was arrived at only after many years of experimentation. It is shared by a number of well-known astrologers; Cheney, one of the best of a couple of generations ago, was outspoken in his denunciation of them. They will not be taken into account in this book.

The more one practices and studies the magnificent art of astrological delineation, the greater respect one develops for the wisdom of the fathers who have handed it down to us. This does not minimize the value of the immense labor of moderns like Leo, Sepharial, Carter and others, who in truly scientific spirit have experi-

mented, classified and analyzed a constant succession
of horoscopes, charting down what appeared to be new
facts, but always working within the great traditional
principles which have never and will never be disproved.
It is along these lines that research will be most productive. The attempts to discredit basic facts, accepted
for ages by astrologers of all schools and nations, may
result in some temporary publicity for the individual
who tries it, but the ancients, whose labors built up this
knowledge, are not likely to turn any handsprings in
their graves because of it. Traditional astrology is too
well-based and well-established. And it is on the principles of traditional astrology applied in the modern
manner but with full deference to its undoubted truth,
that the suggestions made in this book are based.

In setting forth these principles, the "reasons"
behind them will be omitted. This is intended as a
practical work of reference for students as well as pro-
fessionals, and, in fact, for individuals who would not
claim to be either, but who have sufficient elementary
knowledge of astrology to be able to set up and progress
a horoscope and who desire a clear set of reliable rules
formulated which, if they are followed, will yield the
information they seek. There are sound reasons, exoteric
and esoteric, why the MidHeaven has rule over the
occupation, why the Sun governs influence and authority, why the sixth house relates to employment. Others
have set forth these reasons. Here they will be taken for
granted.

Neither will the perennial question of whether the
planets "indicate" or "influence" the things they stand
for be considered. The writer has his own opinion as to

this and has stated it at length in other works, but it would be out of place here. The terms "indicate" and "influence" will be used impartially and interchangeably. The stars and planets certainly act as though they radiate "influences," whether they actually do or not. They also act as "indicators" of conditions, circumstances, qualities or their lack and all the rest of the great horoscopic bill-of-fare. The theory behind it all does not affect the application of the undoubted facts.

And so the principles may now be stated and will be quite readily grasped by all to whom the reading of a horoscope is reasonably familiar.*

Factors to examine in determining vocational possibilities are these:

(1) Planets† (if any) in the tenth house. A planet nearest the MidHeaven normally takes precedence over those further away, though this general rule is subject to a number of modifications which will be explained in the proper place.

(2) A planet in the ninth house but within 5° of the tenth has a tenth as well as a ninth house influence and should be treated as if in the tenth. A planet in the eleventh house but within 5° of the tenth also has a tenth house sway but this is weaker than if in the tenth or ninth. Examine the sign on the cusp, its ruler, the sign and house in which the ruler is found.

(3) Next look for any planet exactly aspecting the MidHeaven. If none, then the planet or planets configured with it by platic (inexact) aspect, if within 5° of orb.

---

* See Appendix A for explanation of symbols.
† Sun and Moon (luminaries) are included as planets to avoid repetition.

(4) If ♄ has not already appeared in one of the above categories, viz., in or within 5° of the tenth, ruling the tenth cuspal sign or aspecting the M.C., he should next be considered, as he is normal planetary ruler of the tenth. Examine the sign he is in.

(5) If ♑ has not similarly appeared, this sign is now up for consideration together with planets occupying it. ♑ is the normal tenth house sign.

(6) This exhausts tenth house factors. We must then look to the sixth house and its affiliates. The sixth house governs employment, whereas the tenth is concerned with the nature of the occupation. In the horoscope of an employee the sixth represents his employers. If and when he becomes an employer himself it then has reference to his employees. "A good servant makes a good master" (or "A bad servant makes a bad master") is literally true astrologically. The same factors largely (but not wholly) govern both. Take planets in the sixth (or in the fifth or seventh if within 5° orb of sixth) in the same way as described in Rule (1).

(7) Take sign on cusp of sixth as in Rule (2). However, planets aspecting the cusp of sixth as in Rule (3) have no influence and are disregarded.

(8) If ☿ has not appeared in applying any of the foregoing Rules, he is next in line for consideration, as normal ruler of the sixth. Follow Rule (4), substituting ☿ for ♄.

(9) The sign ♍ normally governs employment just as ♑ rules occupation. Follow Rule (5) substituting ♍ for ♑.

(10) There are no more factors peculiar to employment. Next on the agenda is the second house which

has to do solely with money, gain, profit and loss. Good configurations between the second, tenth and sixth are excellent for the things ruled by the planets or signs concerned. Follow Rule (1), substituting second house for tenth.

(11) Follow Rule (2) similarly. Rule (3) is ignored as in the case of the sixth house.

(12) If ♀ has not yet appeared she should now be taken, as normal ruler of the second. Follow Rule (4), substituting ♀ for ♄.

(13) Follow Rule (5) substituting ♉ (normal second house sign) for ♑.

(14) Now carefully note down all aspects between planets concerned with tenth, sixth and second houses; also between planets in ♑, ♍, and ♉; finally between ♄, ☿, and ♀.

(15) Examine the planet rising closest to the Ascendant.

(16) Finally take the best planet in the horoscope, if this has not appeared in the foregoing. The question of what constitutes the "best" planet will be exhaustively analyzed in the chapter dealing with this feature exclusively. In general, however, it is the planet most strongly placed by sign, house and elevation, with fewest adverse and greatest number of favorable aspects.

These 16 Rules constitute the principles to be applied in determining (a) the ideal vocation of the native from the standpoint of natural aptitude, (b) the occupations which offer greatest possibilities of financial return; not necessarily the same as (a).

But another problem immediately confronts us.

Should the native be content to remain in the employ of others or should he aim at becoming the head of his own business or profession? It is quite certain that in many cases the horoscope is such that it points to greater success in a well-paid executive position than could possibly be attained as sole owner of a commercial or professional enterprise. Yet there are those who are happiest as "their own boss," with a small income rather than working for someone else for a much larger one. Additional rules for determining this must now be formulated.

(17) Examine the Constitutional groupings of the planets (Cardinal, Fixed, Common). For greatest success in one's own enterprise, there should be a preponderance of the planets and angles in Cardinal signs.

(18) How many planets are Accidentally Dignified (in first, fourth, seventh or tenth houses)?

(19) For high executive positions in the employ of others but not calling for "ultimate" decisions there should be a preponderance of planets in Fixed signs. Examine.

(20) In connection with Rule (19), for best results, Succedent houses (second, fifth, eighth, eleventh) should be well occupied. How many planets are succedently placed?

Finally we come to the question of Partnership. Many a deficient vocational horoscope can be redeemed by selection of a partner who supplies the deficiencies, even though himself lacking in other qualities possessed by the native. Partnership possibilities are to be analyzed as follows:

(21) Planets in the seventh house. Follow Rule (1).

(22) Sign on cusp of seventh. Follow Rule (2). Disregard Rule (3) in relation to seventh.

(23) ♀ rules seventh, through the latter's normal sign, ♎. As ♀ has been analyzed already by reason of its rulership of the second house sign, ♉ , its position, aspects, etc., already taken should be noted again for seventh house consideration.

(24) Follow Rule (5), substituting ♎ for ♑.

(25) For accurate appraisal of the harmony and success of any given partnership, the individual natal horoscopes of the prospective partners should be compared. The technique is set forth in the chapter devoted to "Partners."

When all of these Rules have been conscientiously applied, the Vocational, Employment and Partnership possibilities of the horoscope will have been as completely explored as our present astrological knowledge permits, subject to some amplification which need not be embodied in additional Rules but which will round out the information arrived at by their application.

Thus the Ascendant, the Sun-sign, and to a lesser degree the Moon-sign, show certain aptitudes and success possibilities inherent in the sign. They are subordinate, however, to the distinctively vocational factors embraced by the formulated rules. Also any particularly strong house or sign may have a minor bearing on the analysis, even though in no way linked up with the exclusive occupational or money-making factors.

These are important, because, in very weak vocational charts, the astrologer may be driven to fall back upon these ordinarily subordinate indicators as a last resort.

There remains the question of the best periods in which to undertake to put into effect the recommendations arrived at by the vocational analysis. When is "exactly the right time" to apply for that position, launch that business, open that store? The progressed or "directed" horoscope furnishes the answer.

Each of the above Rules, its application, examples taken from actual horoscopes, and its various modifications will be treated in the chapters which follow.

It will be seen that vocational guidance by astrology cannot be tackled in the lighthearted fashion in which it is often undertaken. It is a serious business, requiring much time and concentration for reliable and effective conclusions to be reached.

Yet after all it is worth the time and effort involved, if there is thereby obtained positive knowledge of the line of endeavor which is most likely to lead the individual to success and happiness.

CHAPTER III

Occupation Rulerships: Planets

BEFORE we can proceed to apply the principles laid
down in Chapter I, it is necessary to have a clear picture
of the planetary and sign rulerships of the myriad occupations open to man. In Astrology we always proceed
from the general to the particular. We ascertain the
principle and reason from that to its many individual
applications. The assignment of any given department
of life to a specific planet is never arbitrary. There is
always a sound underlying reason. And millennia of
observation (except in the case of the three planets, ♅,
♆ and ♇, discovered within the past two centuries)
have borne out the rulership assigned in all cases. In fact
the observation came first—the theory later.

Thus Jupiter governs all things into which the element of abundance enters. Being the great benefic, it
bestows abundance of good in all departments, physical,
mental, spiritual. It rules prosperity on that account,
but it also rules religion, which makes for "the more
abundant life." Yet in affliction it still runs true to
form. It may give adiposity—abundance of flesh. Its
diseases are those of too abundant eating and drinking:
gout, liver and blood ailments, abscesses (swellings),
boils, carbuncles, biliousness and the like.

Jupiter itself is the largest (most abundant) object
in the Solar System except the Sun, which rules "greatness" in other ways. There is always a connection, not

fanciful or far-fetched but extending down into the very heart of being, between the planet or luminary, the things it rules and their relationship to each other. This should be remembered, otherwise a mere superficial recitation of "Things ruled by the planets" may lead the novice to believe that they are just a hodge-podge catalogue of arbitrary groupings without rhyme or reason. Nothing could be further from the truth.

With this understood, we may proceed to classify the various occupations according to their planetary and sign rulerships. The student will need often to refer to these classifications in interpreting his own vocational indicators in the natal chart. For convenience an appendix* is furnished giving the planetary ruler of each occupation in alphabetical order.

It is of course impossible to cover every conceivable line of endeavor followed by the two billion human beings who populate the earth. Of some of these the writer and the reader may never even have heard. It should not be difficult, however, by reference to the underlying basis of each rulership to arrive at the planet, sign and house concerned with any vocation not expressly mentioned.

A business or profession is likely to involve more than its main planetary ruler. Thus the element of "trading," ruled by Mercury may frequently have to be taken into account where buying or selling enters into the picture. Even an artist may need to sell his pictures after painting them. This is not invariable however. It is conceivable that supreme excellence in some profession may be exploited commercially by another individual

*Appendix C.

who has trading talent, though this is wholly absent in the one whose work is thus marketed.

In the case of occupations with multiple rulership, all planets, etc., must be considered. Life insurance has to do with death (♏, eighth house, ♇, ♂). It also is involved with risk or speculation, at least so far as the single insured individual is concerned. (♌, fifth house, ☉). And the contract of insurance brings in still other elements (♊, third house, ♅). These are entirely apart from the principles common to all vocational selection, as set forth in Chapter I. There are still the occupational house, employment house and money house to consider, with the planets and signs that govern them. Also the first house with its peculiar dominance over the energies of the native, and the eleventh with its foreshadowing of the likely sources from which fulfillment of the native's ambitions will come, cannot be ignored. The Part-of-Fortune, too, contributes its moiety to the completed picture.

From all of which it may be gathered that anyone who feels that he can set a pointer to his birth month and drop a penny into a weighing machine, then by reading what is printed on the reverse side of the weight card that drops out determine his occupation, is the victim of acute self-deception.

Planetary vocations follow:*

SUN — ☉

KEYNOTES: Authority, Rule, Command, Power, Importance, Dignity, Government, Gold.

VOCATIONS: Bankers, Presidents, Foremen, Depart-

---

* Where a vocation appears under more than one planet, all govern it.

ment Heads, Stock-Exchange Workers, Stock Spec-
ulators, Investment Bankers, Occupations Involving
Children, Jewelers, Workers in Gold, Heart Special-
ists, Workers in Amber, Impresarios, Entertainment
Directors, Gin Manufacturers (☉ rules the Juniper),
Lion Tamers, Spotlight Operators, Orange Growers,
Park Keepers, Playground Directors, Theatre Owners
and Managers, Walnut Growers.

MOON — ☽

KEYNOTES: Change, Women, Liquids, Real Estate,
The Public, The Secondary, The Temporal.

VOCATIONS: Travelling Men, Sailors, Nurses, Fisher-
men, Liquor Dealers, Laundry Proprietors and
Workers, Cabbage and Cauliflower Growers, Chicken
Fanciers, Cheese Manufacturers, Bath House Pro-
prietors, Bakers, Boat Owners, Brewery Workers,
Brewers, Dairy Farmers, Dairies, Household Help
(Female), Poultry Raisers, Chinaware and Glassware
Manufacturers, Melon Growers, Midwives, Milk-
men, Mushroom Growers, Obstetricians, Plastic
Artists, Restaurant Proprietors and Workers, Tavern
and Taproom Owners and Helpers, Waiters and
Waitresses, Watchmen.

MERCURY — ☿

KEYNOTES: The Mind, Mentality, Memory, Transportation, Documents, Writing, Teaching, Intellect.

VOCATIONS: Clerks, Accountants, Bookkeepers, Writers,
Teachers, Lecturers, Orators, Secretaries, Mail Car-
riers, Bus Drivers, Train Conductors, Architects,
Authors, Acoustic Experts, Bee Keepers, Book-

binders, Actuaries, Correspondents, Typists, Interpreters, Recorders of Deeds, Diplomats, Dietitians,
Errand Boys, File Clerks, Retail Grocers, Governesses, Handwriting Experts, Information Clerks,
Jugglers, Reporters, Messengers, Merchandise Managers, Buyers, Salesmen, Nerve Specialists, Paper
Manufacturers, Editors, Notaries Public, Stenographers, Storekeepers, Stationers, Printers, Publishers, Doctors, Healers, Radio Announcers, Telephone Operators.

VENUS — ♀

KEYNOTES: Love, Beauty, Art, Young Women and
Girls, Music, The Fine Arts, Adornment, Money.

VOCATIONS: Artists, Musicians, Singers, Actors, Toilet
Accessory Makers, Cosmeticians, Beauty Parlor
Operators, Florists, Women's Apparel Manufacturers
and Dealers, Dressmakers, Milliners, Tailors, Con-
fectioners, Maids, Candy Manufacturers, Dry Goods
Stores, Entertainers, Furniture Manufacturers and
Dealers, Hotel Keepers and Workers, Bee Keepers,
Landscape Gardeners, Interior Decorators, Social
Secretaries, Throat Specialists, Perfume Manufac-
turers, Peach Growers, Society Editor, Amusement
Concessionaries, Art Museum Curators, House
Painters and Paperhangers, Photographers, En-
gravers, Illustrators, Cashiers, Tellers, Capitalists,
Pursers, Money Lenders.

MARS — ♂

KEYNOTES: Fires, Quarrels, Energy, Metals, Initiative,
Effort, Pain, Weapons.

VOCATIONS: Soldiers, Army Officers, Pugilists, Assayers, Surgeons, Gun Makers, Butchers, Iron and Steel Workers, Dentists, Barbers, Armament Makers and Workers, Metal Workers, Carpenters, Executives, Firemen, Policemen, Guards, Hardware Manufacturers and Dealers, Implement Makers, Locksmiths, Lumberjacks, Mechanics, Machinists, Stock Raisers, Wrestlers, Occupations connected with things made by fire.

JUPITER — ♃

KEYNOTES: Abundance, Spirituality, Religion, Prosperity, Affluence, Wealth, Law, Publications, Voyages or Long Journeys.

VOCATIONS: Lawyers, Clergymen, Editors, Publishers, Advertising Agents, Ad-Writers, Judges, Woolen Merchants, Wholesale Grocers, Aldermen, Appraisers, Bond Salesmen, Cashiers, Capitalists, Doctors (of Divinity, Literature, Law or Philosophy), Pursers, Financiers, Jockeys, Horse Trainers, Racing Stable Owners and Workers, Law-Court Attachés, Writers for Publication, Sporting Goods Manufacturers and Dealers, Guides, Whale Hunters, Chiropodists, Shoe Manufacturers and Dealers, Shoe Workers.

SATURN — ♄

KEYNOTES: Hardships, Delays, Obstacles, Difficulties, Misfortunes, Poverty, Hard Labor, Tradition, The Well-Established, The Practical, Real Estate, The Old, The Conservative.

VOCATIONS: Miners, Real Estate Dealers, Farmers, Cemetery Lot Salesmen, Excavators, Builders, Con-

tractors, Bricklayers, Gardeners, Tanners, Dealers in
Hides, Leather Goods Manufacturers and Dealers,
Coal and Ice Dealers, Watch and Clock Makers and
Repairers, Laborers, Tombstone Makers, Under-
takers, Efficiency Experts, Priests, Monks, Nuns,
Sextons, Timekeepers, Farm Hands, Grain Dealers,
Plumbers, Night Workers, Night Watchmen, Work-
ers Underground.

URANUS — ♅

KEYNOTES: The New, The Unusual, The Surprising,
Sudden Happenings, Inventions, Advanced Thought.

VOCATIONS: Scientists, Inventors, Astrologers, Occultists, Faith Healers, Chiropractors, Clairvoyants,
Aviators, Automobile Racers, Automobile Manufacturers and Dealers, Automobile and Airplane
Mechanics, Electricians, Radio Manufacturers and
Dealers, Radio Announcers, Moving Picture Producers, Movie Theatre Owners, Garage Proprietors,
Research Workers, Social Service Workers, Telephone Operators, Lighting Specialists, Psychotherapists, Nerve Specialists, Motormen, Metaphysicians,
X-Ray Workers, Electrical Appliance Manufacturers
and Dealers, Instrument Manufacturers and Dealers,
Telegraphers, Lecturers, Engineers.

NEPTUNE — ♆

KEYNOTES: The Mysterious, The Subtle, The Obscure,
The Secret, The Sea, Imagination.

VOCATIONS: Poets, Mind Readers, Musicians, Occult
Writers, Pharmacists, Chemists, Naval Officers, Oil
Workers, Oil Well Operators, Filling Station Owners,

Fish Markets, Anaesthetists, Distillers, Beach Life Guards, Astrologers, Detectives, Private Investigators.

PLUTO — ♇

KEYNOTES: Death, Great Catastrophes, Dictators, General Calamities, World Wars, The Completely New, The Entirely Exclusive.

VOCATIONS: It is hazardous at present to use ♇ as a significator of occupation. His comparatively recent discovery, combined with the obscure nature of the planet, make it advisable to ignore him in vocational selection, except in connection with death and things appertaining to it. Thus he undoubtedly governs Undertakers, Embalmers, Cemetery Associations, Life Insurance Salesmen and other workers, and all occupations connected in any way with the end of life. It is probable that very outstanding success, such as makes the native a world figure, may be due to ability to express Pluto's good aspects. Apparently very few can do this fully, though all appear to be affected by his bad ones.

NOTE: See additional information regarding ♇ in Appendix D.

CHAPTER IV

Occupation Rulerships: Signs

Planets take precedence of signs in respect to occupation, as indeed they do in all departments of life. It is well known that any planet in a house dominates the house, the sign on the cusp being secondary. This law is modified only in the case of the Ascendant. The rising sign marks the native more powerfully (especially as to personal appearance) than any planet in the first house unless such planet be within 5° of the Ascendant, in which case the latter will dominate. This applies even if the planet is at the end of the twelfth house, within 5° orb of the Ascendant.

If no planet is in a house, the sign on the cusp of the house must be examined and considered in conjunction with the planet which rules this sign. In the case of occupation the tenth house sign itself is of considerable moment and it may be possible to arrive at a satisfactory occupation even though the planetary ruler of the sign is afflicted, providing the MidHeaven is well aspected.

It would not be true to say that a sign rules all the things governed by its ruling planet. ♉, for example, is ruled by ♀ but has no dominance whatever over some of the things ♀ governs. It also possesses characteristics of its own, quite foreign to ♀. Thus the latter rules elegance, grace, delicacy, foppishness, all of which are alien to the sturdy, matter-of-fact ♉, but which are found in full measure in ♎︎, the other sign over which ♀ rules. The bulldog nature of ♉︎ and its fighting qualities when once aroused are the very antithesis of the peace-loving characteristics of ♀, itself the planet of peace.

♀, however, rules money and so does ♉︎. Yet ♎︎ has nothing to do with money, and while ♉︎ people usually possess a certain money sense and are shrewd in handling finances, the native of ♎︎ is frequently very impractical in this regard. ♎︎ rules artists, whose improvidence is often marked. These statements, of course, are generalizations only. A ♉︎ native with a poor financial horoscope otherwise could quite easily live a life of want, while a ♎︎ subject with the opposite type of natal chart might end up an international banker. The principle to bear in mind is that each planet has its own characteristics, part of which may be the same as those of the sign or signs it governs but some of which are its own exclusive property.

Some signs follow the qualities of their ruling planets to a much greater degree than others. Thus ☉ possesses almost all the characteristics of its single sign, ♌︎. On the Ascendant it injects both the qualities and something of the appearance of the true ♌︎. The extent to which it swamps out the rising sign depends upon the strength of the latter. Common signs yield right of way very easily to a powerful planet such as ☉ or ♅; cardinal signs less easily; fixed signs are most resistant of all. ♏︎ rising remains ♏︎ rising as a rule, in spite of the impact of an ascending planet, and the latter plays second string.

A good example of the almost complete superseding

of a common sign by a planet on the Ascendant is the horoscope of Franklin D. Roosevelt. Here ♅ is within 2½° of the Virgo Ascendant; ☉ is in ♒, as also ☿ and ♀. The fact of ☉ being in the sign of ♅, ascending planet, gives dominance to the latter which causes it almost completely to nullify the mutable Virgo. Mr. Roosevelt emerges a full-blooded Aquarian with Virgo feebly represented in certain little tricks of manner and perhaps a greater willingness to consult with others than the typical Uranian Ascendant (very dictatorial) ordinarily confers.

The occupational factors need not, however, be read in the same way as the personal characteristics indicated by the Ascendant. A planet on the Ascendant necessarily makes the native a blend of the ascending sign and the planet. One or other may be subordinate or they may be about equal in strength, but there they are and the native has to make the best of them. He may decide to cultivate the qualities of his rising sign and to suppress or mitigate those of his ascending planet, or *vice-versa*. He cannot, however, erase either from his nature.

In the case of a sign or planet concerned with occupation, he has considerable freedom of choice. If the planet is good, he may follow an occupation ruled by the planet and ignore completely the cuspal sign. Or he may try to find a vocation which is governed by both. As a matter of fact, the more of his good planets that are directly or indirectly concerned in the rulership of the occupation he chooses, the better.

Occupations ruled by the signs are given below. To avoid needless repetition, reference is made to the occupational rulerships of the planets where there is duplication of things governed both by the sign and by its ruler.

ARIES — ♈

KEYNOTE: Leadership.

VOCATIONS: Any occupation ruled by ♂ which permits of advancement and promotion. Those with poor chance of advancement should be avoided. Those occupations of ♂ calling for exceptional patience are not for the impatient ♈ unless a good quota of fixed signs are prominent in the chart, or the patient Capricorn or Virgo very strong. Examples of Martian occupations coming under these categories and therefore to be avoided where ♈ is the vocational factor are these: Assayers, Surgeons, Dentists, Carpenters, Lumberjacks, Mechanics. But ♏, also ruled by ♂, has the necessary patience to tackle these non-Arian occupations. ♈, ruling the head, may also denote occupations not governed by ♂, as Hat and Cap Makers or Dealers, Hairdressers or Beauty Parlor Operators. But in the last-named occupations ♀ would also have to be strong. Of itself ♈ is by no means ideal for these professions.

TAURUS — ♉

KEYNOTE: Doggedness.

VOCATIONS: Those occupations of ♀ having to do with money, as Cashiers, Bank Tellers, Capitalists, Pursers, Money Lenders; also Throat Specialists, (if regular medical significators strong). ♉ makes a good Boxer, Soldier or Policeman because of his fighting qualities and his unwillingness to concede defeat. He is excellent as Treasurer of a business or other organization. In these cases ♉ might be the rising sign or Sun Sign, with some other sign or planet more directly concerned with the occupation.

GEMINI — ♊

KEYNOTE: Versatility.

VOCATIONS: Any ruled by ☿ not requiring too much detail and especially those having to do with transportation. ♊ cannot stomach drudgery to the same extent as ☿'s other sign, ♍. Thus normally ♍ makes better office help than ♊ but the latter is the better salesman. ♊ is more curious about *things* and ♍ about *people*. ♊ is inherently much the better speaker and superficially the better writer, but ♍ will be the more thorough in both cases. ♍'s facts are more likely to be right than those of ♊.

Many of ☿'s occupations are common to both ♊ and ♍. *Eliminate* from the former: Teachers, Bee Keepers, Dietitians, File Clerks, Retail Grocers, Governesses, Nerve Specialists, Storekeepers, Doctors, Healers. These are peculiar to ♍, the normal sixth house sign, governing small animals, health and healing, food, and the more humdrum side of ☿'s activities.

CANCER — ♋

KEYNOTE: Domesticity.

VOCATIONS: Those of ☽ insofar as they have to do with the ♋ keynote. Thus Nursing would obviously be a ♋ occupation, but a Traveling Salesman, Fisherman or Tavern Owner would hardly come under that designation.

Of itself ⊕ is greatly concerned with real estate and home ownership, though for best results ♄ should also be strong. Home appliances, house-furnishings and the like are within its guardianship.

LEO — ♌

KEYNOTE: Greatness.

VOCATIONS: Same as ☉ with no exceptions. This may be due to the immense importance of ☉ in the horo-scope as in the Solar System. It apparently dom-inates its only sign, leaving nothing independent for the sign to govern.

VIRGO — ♍

KEYNOTE: Detail.

VOCATIONS: Everything ruled by ☿, not exclusive to ♊, *q.v.* Has especial relationship to service, healing, pets and all mental work involving much detail.

LIBRA — ♎

KEYNOTE: Balance.

VOCATIONS: All those of ♀ not having to do specifically with finance. Vocations it has to do with independ-ently of ♀ are Judges (ruled by ♃ but coming also under ♎ because of the "balanced judgment" of the sign), Diplomats (for same reason), Lawyers—espe-cially Trial Lawyers, owing to ♎'s rulership of opposi-tion. Paradoxical as it may seem, ♀ being the planet of peace, its sign ♎ actually rules war, it being the normal sign of the seventh house which governs public enemies. In this respect ≏ is probably the most inconsistent of the twelve signs.

SCORPIO — ♏

KEYNOTE: Strength.

VOCATIONS: All occupations ruled by ♂ and ♇ except things made by fire, the peculiar property of the fiery sign ♈. Is strong in occupations requiring great patience—where ♈ is weak. Very specially concerned with all occupations having to do with death or things of the dead.

SAGITTARIUS — ♐

KEYNOTE: Publicity.

VOCATIONS: Occupations of ♃ concerned with publicity. *Eliminate* these as peculiar to ♃ or to ♃'s second sign, ♓: Woolen Merchants, Wholesale Grocers, Aldermen, Appraisers, Bond Salesmen, Cashiers, Capitalists, Pursers, Financiers, Whale Hunters, Chiropodists, Shoe Manufacturers and Dealers, Shoe Workers.

CAPRICORN — ♑

KEYNOTE: Hard Work.

VOCATIONS: Occupations of ♄ except Priests, Monks, Nuns, Plumbers, which come under sign rulership of ♓. To ♄'s list of occupations may be added those for which ♑ gives peculiar ability. ♑ is the occupational sign itself. It is the sign of business as such and the distinctive mark of the business man. ♑ excels in those executive positions requiring patience as ♍

excels similarly in subordinate posts calling for the same quality.

AQUARIUS — ♒

KEYNOTE: The Up-To-Date.

VOCATIONS: As Uranus. No exceptions. Also positions which require a friendly personality and skill in meeting the public. ♒ rules friends.

PISCES — ♓

KEYNOTE: Solitude.

VOCATIONS: All vocations of ♆ without exception, and those of ♃ having to do with the feet. Also occupations of solitude as Monks, Nuns, Prison Guards, Wardens; and those connected with large institutions such as Hospitals, Sanitariums, Museums, Libraries, etc. Clubs, Organizations, Secret Societies come under ♓'s rulership, and any occupation connected with these is indicated by ♓ as a vocational sign. If ♀ is strong ♓ often is concerned with musical talent in some direction.

It should always be remembered that the foregoing list, as also the list in Chapter III, is not in itself sufficient as an occupational guide but is only one of the several factors to be taken into account. Without analyzing all of these the occupational adviser will inevitably come to grief. Over-simplification of the problem will lead to nothing but disappointment, but if one has the patience to consider all factors and painstakingly weigh their respective claims one against the other, conclusions of great and lasting value may be drawn which, if followed, should guide the native to the one best vocation for which he is fitted.

CHAPTER V

Planets in the Tenth House

Astrological instructors are familiar with the student who, on learning to set up his horoscope, makes the agonizing discovery that some of his houses contain no planets. He quickly leaps to the conclusion that those departments of life must be blanks for him—that if the second house is empty he will have no money, if the sixth no employment, if the seventh no marriage partner and so on. By this logic, if the fourth and tenth are void of planets he should also have no father and mother, and if the eighth he should never die.

Fortunately Nature does not operate in that way. It is quite true that houses containing planets are likely to bulk more largely in the life than houses containing none. The horoscope is such a complex affair, however, that this can by no means be laid down as a general rule. The planet governing the sign on the cusp of an empty house may be so strongly placed by sign, house and elevation and have so many close aspects or positions to other planets, that it projects the empty house into a position of more importance than some of the full ones.

Therefore, while we first consider planets in the tenth house as the major significators of occupation (as often they are), the student should by no means conclude that if no planets are there this is detrimental to the occupational possibilities.

Thus George Bernard Shaw, who certainly has an

occupation, and one in which he has made a very great success, has no planets at all in his tenth house, (29° ♑ on cusp) though three (☉ from 4° ♌, ♂ from 27½° ♎ and ♅ from 24½° ♉) aspect the MidHeaven. Lord Kitchener, one of England's famous Commanders-in-Chief, who pursued with high distinction the occupation of soldier all his life, has nothing in the tenth (8° ♑ on cusp). Nor are there any planets in aspect to the Mid-Heaven. But ♂, the military planet is in exact △ to the Ascendant (from 22° 47' ♌ to 22° ♈). ♂ is also close △ ☽, which is in 25° 43' ♐. It is likewise △ ♄ in 19° 41' ♈. It is in light △ ♅ in 29° 38' ♈. ♇ is in 29° 30' ♈ and in similar △ to ♂. And ♈, of course, is the sign ruled by ♂. One does not need to have planets in the tenth house to indicate a successful military career, when this kind of Martian set-up exists. And so with any other occupation. Absence of tenth house planets is in no way significant, but their presence calls for first examination where the occupation is concerned.

It also seems to be true that in the natal charts of very outstanding people, the tenth house is likely to be occupied by at least one planet. Thus Adolph Hitler has ♄ there alone. Yet his success (up to this writing) is certainly not due to ♄, which has a □, 4° out of orb, to both ♂ and ♀, the former being reinforced by a P. ♄'s only good aspect is a very light ✳ (7° out) to ♅. Hitler, however, is the most successful (financially) writer in the world. His book, *Mein Kampf*, required reading for every Nazi, has sold millions of copies. The astrological answer is so easy, the most elementary student can perceive it at once. In the third house (writings) in ♑ (intercepted), the tenth house sign, are ☽ and ♃. ☽ has six favorable and no unfavorable aspects and parallels, ♃ has three favorable, no unfavorable aspects and parallels, and ♃ rules publications and rules ♐ the sign of publications which is on the cusp of the third. ☿ which rules writings governs the ninth house (publishing) which has ♊ (sign of writings) on the cusp. ♋ is intercepted in the ninth, and ☽ which rules ♋ is in the third. ☊, very beneficent, is in the ninth, and while ☋ is therefore necessarily in the third, the former governs the sale of the work which is successful beyond the dreams of avarice, while the latter merely indicates that there is something odd or peculiar about the nature of Hitler's written work. Which probably most unbiased or unintimidated people would certainly not deny.

Above is one of the most perfect examples possible of a man who followed the directions of his natal chart in every particular, so far as writing and publishing were concerned, and who reaped a harvest so bountiful as to be almost beyond belief. It is common knowledge that Hitler has long believed in and scrupulously followed the science of astrology.

Other famous personages with occupied tenth houses are Franklin D. Roosevelt, who has ♂ and ☽ there, both unafflicted; Mussolini, with ♅ in close ✶ ♀ and ♃ and exact △ ♆; Lloyd George, ☽ (in eleventh but within 3° orb of tenth) ✶ ♃ exact, ✶ ☉ (2° out) △ ♂ (7° out) and with ☊ in tenth.

It may be of interest to note here that nations have horoscopes and famous nations reflect their horoscopes (or *vice-versa* if one prefers). In the natal chart of

England (Coronation of William the Conqueror, High Noon A.D. 1066), ☉ is right on MidHeaven in 9° 48′ ♑. It has five good aspects or positions—no bad ones. ☿ in 16° 20′ ♑ is in tenth, with four good aspects or positions. ♀ in the eleventh also has a tenth house influence, being less than 2° away, and has an almost exact ✶ ☽—no adverse aspects. The MidHeaven itself has four good aspects, no bad ones.

Therefore while absence of planets in the tenth is in no way adverse to the occupational possibilities, their presence does make for distinction and, if the planets in question have more good aspects than bad and are not adversely placed by sign (in detriment or fall), they are a desirable factor.

Consider then the planet in the tenth house. If more than one, take that one nearest the MidHeaven. A planet in the ninth house within 5° of the tenth exercises a more powerful influence than one actually in the tenth but more than 5° away from the cusp. If two planets both hold the same degree in the tenth, give preference to the one better placed by sign. A planet in exaltation, for instance, over one not so distinguished —or a planet neutral by sign rather than one in detriment. An example may be given from Hitler's chart, though in this case it does not concern the occupational house. ♀ and ♂ are both in 17° ♉ in the seventh house, his house of war.

But ♀ is essentially dignified and ♂ in detriment in ♉. Both are □ ♄ in the tenth. ♀ is the planet of peace, ♂ of war. Peace had her dangers for Hitler but these, because of the fine sign-placement of ♀, were comparatively small. War is infinitely more dangerous to him because of ♂'s evil sign position.

Planets in the same degree should therefore be analyzed with reference to their potentialities for good or evil. In the event of a tie the vote should go to a benefic as against a malefic because of its inherent power for good, apart from the things it signifies. It is impossible to anticipate every condition in a horoscope but the foregoing hints should be comprehensive enough to enable the practitioner or student to reach a decision in any similar situation.

Having decided upon the dominant tenth house planet, observe its aspects. Take every aspect (and position), not forgetting the parallels which so many astrologers slight, but which are of great importance. Ignore minor aspects and regard only the trines, sextiles, oppositions, squares, conjunctions and parallels. If the planet has more bad aspects than good, eliminate and proceed to the next selection. If it has a slight preponderance of good over bad (say 4 to 3), list it as a possibility. If it is exalted or in dignity, this in itself is as good as one or two additional favorable aspects. If it is in detriment or fall, better rule it out unless the proportionate good over bad is very marked—say 6 to 3 or some similar percentage.

Assuming you find a tenth house planet good enough to be considered, your next step is to determine if it has any kind of a hook-up with the second house (money). This may consist of a good aspect to ♀ (normal second house ruler), or to any planet in the second house or to the ruler of the sign on the second house cusp, also to any planet in ♉, the money sign. If none of these

aspects are present, better leave that planet out of
consideration if you wish to make money out of your
occupation. A good aspect of the planet from ♃ or ☉
may be some kind of a substitute for a direct monetary
connection, but for lucrative results it is much better
to have the money planet, house or sign directly concerned. Rather take a second string planet with such
direct hook-up than your first choice, if only a ♃ or
☉ aspect. You can return to the latter if you must,
should the other selections prove to be lacking.

Assuming you have found a satisfactory tenth house
planet with second house connections, another consideration may enter. Are you contemplating obtaining
employment or launching into business for yourself?
In the former case you must consider also if there is any
connection between the tenth and the sixth (employment). If you can also find aspects from the sixth to the
second (money), you are indeed fortunate, but while
this is highly desirable it is not absolutely essential if a
tenth-sixth aspect exists.

Sixth house factors may be any or all of the following:
A good aspect from the planet in the tenth to a planet
in the sixth or to ☿ or to the ruler of the sixth house
cusp, or to any planet in the sign ♍. (☿ is normal ruler
and ♍ normal sign of the sixth house.)

The reader may logically inquire if a sixth-second
house aspect would not be equally good for employment, disregarding the occupational tenth. The answer
is yes, if "just a job" is the requirement. Unless the
tenth is included in the setup, however, the employment is likely to remain only that, with no advancement or recognition and with little or no hope of it ever

leading to the native acquiring a business or profession of his own.

We are now ready to examine the things governed by our first-choice planet as set forth in Chapter III, but before doing so let us note the planet with which our selection is in closest good aspect. If it is in the second, so much the better. It will narrow down our choice of the many things our chosen planet rules. If we can find an occupation ruled by both planets, that is ideal.

Examples will be given in the next chapter.

CHAPTER VI

Ideal Occupational Factors

Let us take our top-ranking occupational planet and, to begin with, assume that the most ideal set of aspects exists to it, as in rare horoscopes may be the case. Once in a blue moon an astrologer comes across such a horoscope. Most of the time, even in the charts of the very successful, while the setup may be quite good, it is far from ideal.

Also ideal astrological layouts must be backed up by the energy of the native himself. Otherwise he will be one of those who, having every opportunity placed in his way, made a mess of things. Of course a weak horoscope in other directions would then be indicated. Many successful people have only Grade B vocational factors in the very occupations in which they have climbed to the top. In that case, however, the planetary placements, groupings by constitution and other vital indicators are such that the immense drive necessary to succeed in the face of difficulties, is astrologically present. Even then these individuals are usually in the best field the horoscope indicates for them.

Consider for instance the occupational factors of John D. Rockefeller, Sr.,* the business genius who started the immense oil industry of the United States. The ideal planet in the tenth house for him would have been ♆ which rules oil well operators, or at least ♅

* For Natal Chart see page 154.

which rules the new (and therefore, in those days, held co-rulership with ♆ over oil). ☽, which governs liquids of any kind, is secondarily concerned. But none of these planets appears in the tenth house or the second. In the tenth are ♂ (in his detriment, ♎) and ♃. In the second no planet appears but ♐ is the sign on the cusp and ♃ (ruler of ♐) is therefore planetary ruler of the second. Ruler of the money house in the vocational house is almost as good as being in aspect to a planet in the house, and remembering that the keynotes of ♃ are *Abundance, Prosperity, Affluence, Wealth* (among other things) we see that we are at once on the track of the astrological reason for the Rockefeller millions.

While ♃ rules prosperity, however, he has nothing to do directly with oil. Yet he has a close hookup with ♆ who does rule it—an almost exact △, the best aspect in the horoscope. ♆ is in the third house (the mind), making Mr. Rockefeller "oil minded." It is in ♒, sign of ♅, the other oil ruler—a very significant placement. We do therefore have our second house involvement in oil even though it is a trifle roundabout, due to the △ of the second house ruler to ♆. We also note that ♃ has a light △ to ☽, which is in the partnership house (seventh). Rockefeller benefited through partners, but he was always the driving force behind them. ♆ is also △ ☽, somewhat closer. ♇, a very potent planet in making millionaires if other configurations favor, is also △ ♆ from the fifth house (speculation—which the sinking of oil wells certainly is).

For good measure the secondary planet in the tenth, ♂, which we decided to ignore, is △ ♆ too. It is also in almost exact ✳ ♄ (business planet). ♃ is ✳ ♄ as well.

We may take note likewise of ☉'s ⚹ MC. ☉ rules influence from those of higher station and such influence was exercised early in Rockefeller's career to his great benefit.

Turning to the other side of the picture we find that afflictions of the direct occupational significators are few and insignificant. The worst is a □ of ☽ to ♅, exact within 2°. There is a very light ☍ of ♅ to MC. Outside of these only ♄ □ ♀ offers any real obstacle. Rockefeller had difficulties in plenty to encounter. Not the least were the Government prosecutions of Standard Oil, involving his companies in litigation extending over many years. ♉ is on the cusp of his seventh house which therefore is ruled by ♀. This planet normally governs the seventh house in any case and therefore is undisputed ruler of this house of litigation in Rockefeller's chart. ♄, governing everything of a long-drawn-out nature, clearly indicates the type of legal difficulties by which he would be harassed. Yet so overwhelming are the favorable aspects that the damage done to him either mentally, physically or financially was entirely negligible.

This horoscope has been used as an example because it belongs to the most successful industrialist of the last century, to a man long since retired and now dead, and whose career may therefore be viewed in proper perspective.

Certainly the four good aspects, no bad ones to ♆ and its close connection with the second and tenth houses, even though not quite direct, paint a perfect picture of a successful oil magnate. There are other supporting features we have not even touched upon

such as ♅ in ♆'s sign, ♓, while ♆ is in ♅'s sign, ♒;
the benefic ☊ ♂ ♅ (though ☋ is in the tenth, account-
ing for the severe criticism and attacks to which Rockefeller was subjected for his business methods; also
indicating that those business methods were not altogether of sweetness and light).

Mr. Rockefeller, of course, had the tremendous drive
of his ♏ Ascendant coupled with the extreme tenacity
of his ⊕ ☉. It may be asserted that no one could have
made those Neptunian aspects pay greater dividends
than did he. With a weak Ascendant and Sun sign, the
bad aspects might have left him a mere mediocrity. It
took power to accomplish what he did, in spite of the
favoring occupational factors—and he had what it took.

With this digression we may proceed to analyze our
tenth house and second house planetary aspects. Assuming something that rarely occurs—the ideal—let us
suppose that ♃ in his own sign, ♐ (essentially dignified)
is in the tenth, △ ♀ essentially dignified in her own
house, ♉. An intercepted sign would be necessary for
such an aspect but this is an occurrence of great fre-
quency in these latitudes. Such a set of positions and
aspects is so extraordinarily good (and rare) that,
given a first-class supporting horoscope, the native
would be likely to make a success of almost any business
or profession he tackled. However we must get down
to cases.

Referring to occupations governed by ♃ (Chapter
III), we find we have a choice of between 30 or 40.
♀ gives us as many or more. Our question is, "Have
these two planets any vocations in common?" If so we
have narrowed our choice, at least in the first instance,

to some business or profession, smiled on by both. We must bear in mind that ♃ is in ♐, not its other sign of ♓ and that therefore the Piscean occupations are not to be considered. See Chapter IV for these. Also that ♀ is in ♉, not ♎. Its money rulership therefore is paramount rather than its artistic side. What then does ♃ govern, most akin to money? The list offers us the choice of several things; Appraisers, Bond Salesmen, Cashiers, Capitalists, Pursers, Financiers. The Venusian list gives us Cashiers, Tellers, Capitalists, Pursers, Money Lenders. Three of these appear in both lists: Cashiers, Capitalists, Pursers.

Now obviously unless a boy leaving school or college is a scion of a very wealthy family, he cannot exactly select "Capitalist" as an occupation. If he is the son of a J. P. Morgan partner that may be a possible career, but to less favored mortals, a more modest ambition, at least at the outset, is indicated. The interpretation must be made with common sense, but if ♀ and ♃ are unafflicted (no or very few bad aspects as compared with their good ones), and there are no strong afflictions to planets in ♉ (money sign) or in the second (money) house, the course is quite clear.

Put that youngster, boy or girl, into some occupation where he or she will have the handling of money and then let him find himself. He may start as a humble assistant in the cashier's cage and, if he measures up to the quite reasonable possibilities of his natal chart, wind up as Treasurer of the Company. Ultimately he may really turn out to be a financier, capitalist or investment banker. But start him off in something which will give play to his inborn money instinct. Nature will take its course if he coöperates.

It must be borne in mind that the primary objective is not merely to place the native in some calling which is ruled by a good planet in the tenth (if such there be). The number of vocations each planet governs is very large and may differ widely from each other. Consider for instance the difference in temperament required by a policeman and a barber. Yet both are ruled by ♂. Clergymen and whale hunters are seemingly two professions with nothing in common (if we may leave Jonah out of it). ♃, however, rules the life-work of both. What could be less poetic than a fish market? ♆ governs poets and also fish markets.

It is not one planet alone, no matter how excellent may be its sign position and aspects, which gives the clue to the native's vocational abilities, but the nature of the planet or planets with which it is in closest aspect—their sign positions, house positions and aspects. And for financial success, the second house, when connected with the first in some manner by aspect or position of planets in both or planets ruling both, is of first importance.

We considered above an example of tenth-second planets having so much in common that it was an easy task to decide on the calling which would provide the greatest opportunities for success. Other harmonious combinations with similar possibilities may now be listed.

☉—♂: Because ☉ rules Authority and ♂ Executives, such a tenth-second combination points strongly to the training of the native for a governing position, rather than that of a subordinate. This would be particularly the case if cardinal signs were in the majority.

☿ — ♅ : An ideal occupation would be a Radio Announcer which both planets jointly govern.

♀ — ♄ : The former rules Art—the latter Building. A tenth-second combination obviously points to architecture as an indicated profession.

♅ — ♆ : Both planets have rulership over the Occult. An occupation touching any phase of this is immediately up for consideration where these two planets connect from tenth to second in good aspect.

These few examples will perhaps convey an idea of the principle involved in tenth-second house occupational selection. Which particular planet is in the tenth and which in the second may or may not be a matter of consequence. It depends upon the house for which the planet has the greatest affinity. Thus in the ♀ — ♄ example given above, it would obviously be a better setup if ♀ were in the second, ♄ in the tenth. ♀ is normal ruler of the second due to its government of ♉, the sign previously identified with the second house. Similarly, ♄, ruler of ♑, regular tenth house sign, is well posited therein. Neither is antagonistic to the house of the other. ♄ has no special affinity nor repulsion to ♉, nor has ♀ to ♑. The connection would still be worth consideration if ♄ were in the second and ♀ in the tenth, but it would not possess the outstanding possibilities of ♀ in second, ♄ in tenth.

Astrological analysis is largely a matter of common sense. Nature has made her occupational signposts very clear and has laid down precise laws by which they may be deciphered. Given a planet in the tenth and one in the second in good aspect to each other, and both planets exercising rulership over the same occupation or profession, and a first choice clearly presents itself. Complications, such as more than one planet in either house, can be resolved by eliminating the weaker planets and concentrating on the strongest. If it be remembered that fall and detriment are weakness, exaltation and dignity strength, that planets in the houses of their signs or exaltations are strong, opposite them weak; if it be held in mind that the nearer a planet is to the cusp, the more dominance it exercises, and finally that a planet which is the ruler of the Ascendant or Sun Sign is stronger than one which has no such rulership, it should not be difficult to apply the foregoing rules.

Seldom, however, is the horoscope such that the ideal calling can be arrived at with such beautiful ease. Only one natal chart in a very great number is likely to have tenth-second significators so clean-cut that the hunt for occupational factors may stop right there. Often one or both houses are empty, or, when occupied, the planets concerned appear to have nothing whatever in common. What are we to do then?

CHAPTER VII

Tenth-second Planets Having
No Common Rulerships

THE law governing planets in good aspect to each other from the tenth to second houses and both ruling some similar vocation, is so clear it can hardly be misconstrued. Suppose, however, we find that the two planets concerned appear to have nothing in common, what is the next procedure? The difficulty is more in seeming than in reality, for as Nature, in the physical world, brings together the most unlikely elements and by combining them produces new substances having qualities possessed separately by neither, so do differing planets in the horoscope act upon each other similarly when in good aspect.

We saw, in the last chapter, how a ♀ — ♄ configuration would behave to produce a talent for architecture. ♄ of itself is no artist. It is inherently very unbeautiful. It is the planet of privation and its forms are stunted and cramped. Yet ♄ takes immense pains. It is the hardest working of all the planets and by far the most patient. It "can wait and not be tired by waiting." "Its outlines," says Sepharial, "are hard and clearcut." Certainly it possesses qualities of great value to the artist.

♀ has little or nothing in common with the labor of putting up a building. ♀ is graceful, elegant, averse to soiled hands, coarse manners, loud talk, manual toil —all of which are much in evidence in the building trades. Yet buildings should be artistic as well as utilitarian. The "four walls and a door" of ♄ without any influence of ♀, may evolve into the divine beauty of the Taj Mahal, the Rheims Cathedral or the Capitol at Washington, when ♀ adds its mellowing touch. It is significant that ♄, great malefic as he is, is exalted in ♎, artistic sign of ♀, the lesser benefic. Yet ♀ finds her exaltation in a sign of ♆ and ♃.

We should not therefore too confidently decide that any two planets are so remote from each other in nature that they have nothing in common or that their blending may not produce valuable talent for some occupation. At first sight ♀ and ♄ appear to be as opposite as any two planets in the Solar System. Yet we have seen how they may work together for good. And the fact that ♀ is exalted in ♄'s sign gives us a lead as to how we may first track down the significance of blended planets.

By taking a planet harmonious enough with another in essence to find exaltation in the other's sign, it is not unlikely that we can deduce suitable occupations from the blend if we apply common sense methods. Let us see.

☉ is exalted in ♈, sign of ♂. We noted in the last chapter the affinity of these two planets for each other.

☽ is exalted in ♉, money sign of ♀. A tenth-second hookup between the two would be better with ☽ in the second rather than in the tenth. The latter house is normally ruled by ♑, in which sign ☽ is in Detriment.

♀ is not evilly affected here, however, while ☽ in the second house of its exaltation sign, is excellent.

Now ☽ rules women and ♀ young women and girls. The two planets, therefore, shed exactly the right combination of influences on any of the several occupations listed under ♀, which primarily concern women. Without covering them exhaustively, as the reader can readily do this for himself, a few typical callings may be cited: Toilet Accessory Makers, Cosmeticians, Beauty Parlor Operators, Women's Apparel Manufacturers and Dealers, Dressmakers, Milliners, Perfume Manufacturers.

☿ is exalted in ♒, sign of ♅. A combination of the two formed one of the examples in the last chapter. Any ultra-modern method of transportation would be indicated by this blend as Aviation, the Automobile Industry, Radio (which transports sound through space), Telephone and Telegraph (which transport speech or information).

♀ is exalted in ♓, sign of ♆ and ♃. Music, which is one of the fine arts ruled by ♀ generally, is definitely under dominion of ♆. Occupations connected with the Manufacture or Sale of Women's Shoes are under the combined rule of ♀ and ♃.

♂ is exalted in ♑, sign of ♄. Both planets are malefics but also rule certain callings. They are likely to be of the strenuous kind because of the sturdy nature of these two planets. We do not find any occupation mentioned in both lists but ♄ has obvious affinity for some of the industries listed under ♂ and *vice-versa*. Thus Contractors, ruled by ♄, have much to do with Carpenters, a ♂ craft, and a favorable configuration of the two by tenth-second house would be an excellent indication of success in that line.

♃ is exalted in ♋, sign of ☽. There is no direct joint rulership of any occupation, but ♃ in ♋ in the second trine ☽ in tenth is one of the finest signs of general financial success to be found in a horoscope. Given a good supporting chart and the native would have to play his cards very badly indeed to make a financial or occupational failure of his life. Nature has started him out with a deck heavily stacked in his favor. Any occupation either of ♃ or ☽ may be followed with good assurance of success.

♄ is exalted in ♎, sign of ♀. This blend was also used as an example in the last chapter. ♄ and ♀ also make a powerful combination for the conservation of money. It usually is made the "hard" way (by working for it), but is tenaciously clung to after being amassed. This is a good aspect for the financial officer of a business or other organization.

♅ is exalted in ♏, sign of ♇ and ♂. Crematoriums would fall to the rulership of a connection between ♅ and ♇ or ♅ and ♂. As between the two latter any occupation connected with very modern machinery would be indicated. ♇ would be concerned with all recently perfected instruments of death: Tanks, Bombers, Munitions generally. Slaughter on a large scale would be his specialty, while ♂ would be likely to rule the more retail methods of killing. All rulerships assigned to ♇ are more or less surmise, due to the relatively short time which has been available for observation of his effects.

It is remarkable, however, and a tribute to the exactness of astrology as a science, how closely astrologers, working independently of each other, agree as to the nature of this newly discovered planet.

♆, as yet, has been assigned no exaltation. Several have been suggested—♌ for one, on the ground that it is not the exaltation sign of any other planet. No planet is exalted in ♍, ♊, or ♐, though ☊ and ☋ are said to be exalted respectively in the two last named. Some astrologers consider ♍ as exaltation sign of ☿. However, ☿ is essentially dignified in ♍ and it is difficult to see how a planet can be exalted and essentially dignified in the same sign. The author's opinion is decidedly that ☿ is exalted in ♒. He inclines to the belief that ♆'s exaltation sign is ♋, even though ♃ is also exalted there. ♆ in good aspect to ☽ makes a nice combination. The two have much in common. Certainly a tenth-second hookup between the two would have excellent possibilities along occupational lines.

Note that one of the Keynotes of ☽ is Liquids, and that ♆ governs occupations having to do with oil. An obvious choice of occupations would be suggested by the two in good aspect.

♇'s exaltation is also at present a mystery and not even a guess can be hazarded.

As may be seen, it is not difficult to decide on occupations suitable to the nature of two planets in good aspect from tenth to second even though they rule nothing in common, providing they are harmonious to each other. When one of the planets is exalted in the other planet's sign, such harmony is to be inferred.

Suppose, however, that the reverse is the case and

one planet is in its fall in the sign ruled by the other, what then?

We may eliminate ☉ and ♀ (☉ in fall in ♀ sign ♎) as no tenth-second aspect could be made between them — ♀ never gets that far away from ☉.

For the same reason we need not consider ☉ and ☿ (☿ in fall in ☉ sign ♌) or ☿ and ♀ (♀ in fall in ☿ sign ♍).

But ☽ is often △ ♂ from tenth to second or *vice-versa*. And ☽ is in fall in ♂ sign, ♏. Also ♂ is exalted in ☽'s detriment, ♑. There would seem, therefore, on the face of it to be considerable antipathy between these two. Yet ☽ in good aspect to ♂ from any point in the chart is known to improve the vitality and give courage, enterprise, an adventurous spirit and much capability.

In many respects these two significators are opposites. Thus ♂ rules Fire, ☽ Liquids; ♂ governs Soldiers, ☽ Sailors; ♂ Executives, ☽ Household Help; and similar opposed occupations.

In such a case (♂ △ ☽—tenth to second) we have to consider the attributes of one of the planets—the type of influence it radiates—rather than the occupations it governs, and select the occupations governed by the other planet with which its qualities seem best to blend.

It is obviously better to have ♂ in tenth (the normal house of ♑) than in second (normal house of ♉) and to have ☽ in second than in tenth. While the houses cannot exactly be said to influence the planets to the same degree as the signs, yet a house, the normal sign of which is the exaltation or dignity of a planet, is certainly better for that planet than one whose normal sign represents its fall or detriment. However, we have to take the planets, signs and houses as they come, and whatever planet happens to be in the tenth, whether well or ill placed, is ordinarily a stronger significator of the occupation than one in the second.

We should therefore consider as representative of the calling the tenth house planet, and, if no occupation common to both it and the planet in the second which it aspects favorably exists, then study the type of influence the second house planet radiates and see how this seems to affect the various occupations of the other planet.

Thus ♂ (from tenth) △ ☽ (in second) poses the question, What Martian occupations are most responsive to lunar vibrations? Examine the keynotes of ☽. These are: Change, Women, Liquids, Real Estate, The Public, The Secondary, The Temporal.

Almost every Martian vocation perhaps has a little something to do with one or other of the above, but there is nothing outstandingly akin in any of them. Thus a soldier might experience frequent changes of location, or he might not. There is no real hook-up. An Army Officer might be in a department of the Government having to do with the leasing or renting of ground for army maneuvers, barracks and the like, but this is not an occupation which can well be *selected*. It might quite easily fall to the lot of a military officer having ☽ in second △ ♂ in tenth but ☽'s influence on ♂ is not very discernible in military affairs. Policemen, who come in contact with the public to a much greater extent than soldiers, are far more responsive to this keynote of ☽ than the latter.

Barbers, likewise are dependent on public contacts

for success, but in their case ♀ which rules personal grooming should be strong. In a soldier's horoscope this is not so necessary. It is true he must be smart and neat in appearance, but if ♀ has not given him these qualities naturally, his top sergeant will do it for him.

No attempt is here made to apply all of ☽'s keynotes to all Martian occupations. The above examples are intended only as a guide. Once the principle is grasped it can be readily adapted to whatever planetary, sign and house positions may exist.

It may be here stated that such grasping of principles and the ability to apply them is the true mark of the competent astrologer. The student or practitioner who relies on "catalogues" listing the meaning of aspects, sign and house positions etc., does not clearly understand the basic fundamentals of the science. He will be in a perpetual quandary because of "conflicts" between one aspect or position and another or several others. He is likely to find the horoscope apparently blowing hot and cold at the same time.

It is necessary that there be such lists, and exceptionally fine, painstaking work of this nature has been done by a variety of Astrological experts. Interpretation, however, is based on principles, not lists. The lists have merely grown out of the principles.

In the case of ☽ (and also of ☉ and of the ruler of the horoscope) it is not so necessary as with other planets to trace a definite type of influence harmonious to the other planet with which it is in aspect. ☽ of itself is ruler of the personality and if it appears in second △ a planet in tenth it is a good indicator of success for any occupation of the other planet, even though none

of its keynotes can readily be applied to such occupation. If one or more of them can be applied so much
the better.

♅ △ ♀ is a very good example of two planets, one
of which is in fall in the other's sign. The fall of ♅ is
♉, ruled by ♀. It is better for ♀ to be in the second
and ♅ in tenth as second's normal sign is ♉. We do
find occupations which, while not ruled by both, fit in
surprisingly well with both. Thus ♀ rules Music, ♅
Radio. ♀ rules Actors, ♅ Moving Pictures. But note
these pertain to the ♎ side of ♀, in which sign ♅ is not
badly placed, rather than to ♉, the money side. Very
satisfactory occupational guidance is given by the
♅-♀ combination including, in addition to the above,
Photographers, Airplane Designers (Airplane plus Art),
Spotlight Operators (Lighting Specialists plus Theatre)
and many others not specifically listed but which can
be deduced from the inherent nature of the two planets
concerned.

For ready reference the affinity or aversion of the
planets for each other is indicated in the following
table:

☉ and ☽:	Neutral.
{ ☉ and ♂:	☉ exalted in ♂'s dignity, ♈.
FRIENDLY	
☉ and ♃:	Neutral.
{ ☉ and ♄:	☉ exalted in ♄'s fall, ♈.
UNFRIENDLY	♄ in detriment in ☉'s dignity, ♌.
{ ☉ and ♅:	☉ in detriment in ♅'s dignity, ♒.
UNFRIENDLY	♅ in detriment in ☉'s dignity, ♌.

☉ and ♆ :   Neutral. (♆'s exaltation and fall un-
                       known.)

☉ and ♇ :   Neutral. (♇'s exaltation and fall un-
                       known.)

The "Unfriendliness" of the planets so labeled to
each other is not to be taken too literally. In good
aspect such planets will work for wholly favorable ends.
The descriptions are comparative only and to aid in
determining, where several second-tenth aspects are
present, which are the most favorable. As the above
table shows, if other things are equal, the following
should be the order of preference:

1. ☉-♂ :   Friendly.
2. ☉-☽; ☉-♃; ☉-♆; ☉- ♇ :   Neutral.
3. ☉-♄ ; ☉-♅ :   Unfriendly.

———————

☽ and ☿ :   Neutral.

{ ☽ and ♀ :
FRIENDLY }   ☽ in exaltation in ♀'s dignity, ♉.

{ ☽ and ♂ :
UNFRIENDLY }   ☽ in detriment in ♂'s exaltation, ♑.
               ♂ in detriment in ☽'s dignity, ♉.

{ ☽ and ♃ :
FRIENDLY }   ♃ exalted in ☽'s dignity, ♋.

{ ☽ and ♄ :
UNFRIENDLY }   ☽ in detriment in ♄'s dignity, ♑.
               ♄ in detriment in ☽'s dignity, ♋.

{ ☽ and ♅ :
UNFRIENDLY }   ♅ exalted in ☽'s fall, ♏.
               ☽ exalted in ♅'s fall, ♉.

☽ and ♆ :   Neutral.

{ ☽ and ♇ :
UNFRIENDLY }   ☽ in fall in ♇'s dignity, ♏.
               ♇ in fall in ☽'s exaltation, ♉.

Order of preference:

1. ☽-♀ ; ☽-♃ :   Friendly.
2. ☽-☿ ; ☽-♆ :   Neutral.
3. ☽-♂;☽-♄ ; ☽-♅ ; ☽-♇ :   Unfriendly.

☿ and ♂ :   Neutral.

{ ☿ and ♃ :   ☿ in dignity in ♃'s detriment, ♍.
{ UNFRIENDLY   ♃ in dignity in ☿'s detriment, ♐.

{ ☿ and ♄ :
{ FRIENDLY   ☿ exalted in ♄'s dignity, ♒.

{ ☿ and ♅ :
{ FRIENDLY   ☿ exalted in ♅'s dignity, ♒.

{ ☿ and ♆ :   ☿ in detriment in ♆'s dignity, ♓.
{ UNFRIENDLY   ♆ in detriment in ☿'s dignity, ♍.

☿ and ♇ :   Neutral.

Order of preference:

1. ☿-♄ ; ☿-♅ :   Friendly.
2. ☿-♂ ; ☿-♇ :   Neutral.
3. ☿-♃ ; ☿-♆ :   Unfriendly.

{ ♀ and ♂ :   ♀ in dignity in ♂'s detriment, ♉.
{ UNFRIENDLY   ♀ in detriment in ♂'s dignity, ♈.

{ ♀ and ♃ :
{ FRIENDLY   ♀ exalted in ♃'s dignity, ♓.

{ ♀ and ♄ :
{ FRIENDLY   ♄ exalted in ♀'s dignity, ♎.

{ ♀ and ♅ :   ♀ in detriment in ♅'s exaltation, ♏.
{ UNFRIENDLY   ♅ in fall in ♀'s dignity, ♉.

{ ♀ and ♆ :
{ FRIENDLY   ♀ exalted in ♆'s dignity, ♓.

{ ♀ and ♇ :   ♀ in dignity in ♇'s detriment, ♉.
{ UNFRIENDLY   ♀ in detriment in ♇'s dignity, ♏.

Order of preference:

1. ♀-♃; ♀-♄; ♀-♆:   Friendly.
2. ♀-♂; ♀-♅; ♀-♇:   Unfriendly.

⎰♂ and ♃:   ♂ in fall in ♃'s exaltation, ⊗.
⎱UNFRIENDLY   ♃ in fall in ♂'s exaltation, ♑.
⎰♂ and ♄:   ♂ exalted in ♄'s dignity, ♑.
⎱NEUTRAL   ♄ in fall in ♂'s dignity, ♈.

(These two malefics are the only pair of planets both Friendly and Unfriendly to each other. May be considered as Neutral on account of this offset.)

⎰♂ and ♅:
⎱FRIENDLY   ♂ in dignity in ♅'s exaltation, ♏.

♂ and ♆:   Neutral

⎰♂ and ♇:
⎱FRIENDLY   ♂ in dignity in ♇'s dignity, ♏.

Order of preference:

1. ♂-♅; ♂-♇:   Friendly.
2. ♂-♄; ♂-♆:   Neutral.
3. ♂-♃:   Unfriendly.

⎰♃ and ♄:   ♃ exalted in ♄'s detriment, ⊗.
⎱UNFRIENDLY   ♄ in dignity in ♃'s fall, ♑.

♃ and ♅:   Neutral.

⎰♃ and ♆:
⎱FRIENDLY   ♃ in dignity in ♆'s dignity, ♓.

♃ and ♇:   Neutral.

Order of preference:

1. ♃-♆:   Friendly.
2. ♃-♅; ♃-♇:   Neutral.
3. ♃-♄:   Unfriendly.

$\left\{ \begin{array}{l} ♄ \text{ and } ♅: \\ \text{Friendly} \end{array} \right.$ ♄ in dignity in ♅'s dignity, ♒.

♄ and ♆:   Neutral.

♄ and ♇:   Neutral.

Order of preference:

1. ♄-♅:   Friendly.
2. ♄-♆; ♄-♇: Neutral.

♅ and ♆:   Neutral.

$\left\{ \begin{array}{l} ♅ \text{ and } ♇: \\ \text{Friendly} \end{array} \right.$ ♅ exalted in ♇'s dignity, ♏.

Order of preference:

1. ♅-♇: Friendly.
2. ♅-♆:   Neutral.

♆ and ♇:   Neutral

Order of preference: None.

For instant use a summary of the foregoing is given below:

Symbols: F = FRIENDLY; U = UNFRIENDLY; N = NEUTRAL; O = OMITTED (as making no major aspects).

	☉	☽	☿	♀	♂	♃	♄	♅	♆	♇
☉		N	O	O	F	N	U	U	N	N
☽	N		N	F	U	F	U	U	N	U
☿	O	N		O	N	U	F	F	U	N
♀	O	F	O		U	F	F	U	F	U
♂	F	U	N	U		U	N	F	N	F
♃	N	F	U	F	U		U	N	F	N
♄	U	U	F	F	N	U		F	N	N
♅	U	U	F	U	F	N	F		N	F
♆	N	N	U	F	N	F	N	N		N
♇	N	U	N	U	F	N	N	F	N	

CHAPTER VIII

The "Best" Planet

Occasionally it happens that all occupational factors are so inferior that the astrologer is almost ready to throw up his hands in despair of finding any planet, sign or house which offers reasonable hope of vocational success. Wherever he turns it is the same story. If planets are in the tenth, second or sixth they are so badly afflicted, so weakly placed by sign, they rather indicate failure than success.

A similar state of affairs prevails in relation to the business (♑), money (♉) and employment (♍) signs. If planets are found therein they appear to be worthless. The planetary rulers of these departments, ♄ , ♀ and ☿ respectively, likewise offer not the least encouragement.

In other words it seems that entry into the business or professional world is barred by a planetary and sidereal chorus chanting "He shall not pass."

This assumes, of course, a well-nigh impossible state of affairs. Almost always some one planet, sign or house at least, which has more good aspects than bad, more strength than weakness, is present. Our task then is comparatively easy. We merely follow that particular indicator to the exclusion of others and select what seems to be the most logical calling or callings, based on its placement by house or sign or by its best aspects with other planets.

We are here considering, however, an extreme case. All indicators even remotely concerned with occupation have to be rejected. What are we to do then? Must we advise the unfortunate native that there is nothing left for him to do but go on relief? Must we tell him, "There is no place for you in industry, the professions or the arts. You are just an occupational misfit?"

Any astrologer who so misused his knowledge certainly should be read out of his honorable calling. There are no "impossible" situations in the horoscope. There is always a way out if one will painstakingly seek for it and not jump to the conclusion that none exists.

The way out in the case of the "hopeless" occupational chart we are theoretically analyzing is *to select the best planet, even though it has not a single occupational connection*. It may be in a house and sign apparently far removed from the three main departments which normally govern this field (tenth-second-sixth). No matter—take it anyway. Then look for some indirect connection and almost always one will be found. Thus the "best" planet may be in the seventh house or the sign Libra. Good enough! Then partnership is indicated as the way out of the *impasse*. If in the first, the native's own efforts will have to supply the missing astrological factors—as indeed they will, no matter where the planet is. Particularly, however, is this indicated by a first house position.

In the third the mind will play the greatest part. The native will have to plan and scheme to overcome the undoubted difficulties before him. The fourth brings the home into some kind of relationship with the occupation, if a planet in the fourth or ruling the fourth is to be the guiding occupational star. Perhaps the work or profession, whatever it is, can best be carried on at home or possibly it has to do with house-to-house work of some kind. The fifth, of course, is likely to bring children into the picture—doubtless a line selling or catering to children or where children play a part. Teaching children might be the solution, but not unless the horoscope has abundance of planets or angles in fixed signs, bestowing the required patience.

The eighth gives a clue to the fact that a silent partner investing money with the native may give him his great chance (eighth rules the partner's money). In the ninth the "best" planet would seem to recommend going abroad or at least a long distance from the birth-place for success. The advertising and publishing fields are likewise a possibility. The eleventh points to friends as the avenue from which help in the upward climb may come, while the twelfth inevitably suggests institutional aid of some nature.

Of necessity these suggestions are very sketchy. A 20-volume work would hardly suffice to list the infinite number of possibilities which the millions of possible horoscopic combinations hold in the occupational line as elsewhere. The native must use his knowledge of the inherent nature of the planets, signs and houses as given in this work or which he has learned elsewhere, to arrive by a process of analysis and elimination at the most suitable avenue to success. No set of examples can possibly be exhaustive.

It need not be disguised that in the case of a lone planet, selected because it is "the best of a bad lot," the fight for a competence is likely to be hard and pro-

longed. Success for the native will be no "pushover."
But by following his star and supplying the missing
elements out of his own strenuous endeavors, he may
in the hilly journey develop a character far stronger
and more worthwhile than a native with the "ideal"
occupational set-up.

We still have to deal with the rare case of a horoscope
which has no planets free from affliction or with a preponderance of good aspects over bad. Or with the even
rarer instance of a chart where every planet has only
adverse configurations—no favoring ones anywhere.
The latter case is next to impossible. In such event it is
doubtful if the native would have survived infancy.
Theoretically, however, there is a bare possibility of
such occurrence, and as this work aims at astrologically
recognizing every type of vocational problem which
could confront anyone, it takes cognizance of even the
remotest problem which might present itself. Nothing
is more annoying than to consult a book purporting to
offer comprehensive advice in a specialized field only
to find that your particular difficulty seems to have
completely escaped the attention of the author, as he
entirely ignores it.

The answer to the question, "What shall I do if I
have no unafflicted planet?" is "Take the least afflicted."
If several seem to tie for that distinction, then take the
one best placed by sign. A planet in exaltation is obviously stronger for good than a planet in detriment or
fall or even neutrally placed. In this writer's opinion
(not shared by all astrologers) exaltation is slightly
better than essential dignity, and fall slightly worse
than detriment. If no planets are dignified or exalted,

then give preference to one neutrally placed as against others in detriment or fall. If such distinctions do not exist then consider the house. While a planet in the normal house of the sign in which it is exalted or dignified is by no means as strong as if in the sign itself, it is still a little stronger than if in a neutral house. Thus ☉ is well placed in the first or fifth (♈ and ♌ houses) and not so well placed in the seventh or eleventh (♎ and ♒ houses). ☿ is nicely posited in the third, sixth or eleventh (♊, ♍, ♒) and adversely so in the ninth, twelfth or fifth. ☿'s disability in the twelfth is more pronounced than elsewhere, probably because of the opposition to the employment and health house.

Yet always there must be some planet a little less badly afflicted than the rest, even in the worst of nativities. And that planet is in a sign and a house and these themselves furnish the clue to the occupation which offers the greatest possibilities for success. Here is a note of hopefulness for the native who "never had a chance" because of his terrifically afflicted horoscope. Nature gives everyone a chance if she allows them to enter the world at all. There is always a way out. It is the tragedy of our educational system that it devotes endless attention to preparing youth for the battle of life and ignores the one sure guide furnished by the natal chart.

Some succeed in finding their ideal calling (sometimes after years of misfit labor) without knowing that astrology could have placed them in their proper niche at the very outset. Others drop into the grave after unhappy lives spent in occupations Nature never intended for them. A few, with exceptional horoscopes, are attracted to their right sphere with little effort on their own part. An infinitesimal percentage, by sheer will-power, make good in the "wrong" vocation and never know the difference. But how much more they might have accomplished, successful as they are, had they followed the natural occupational lines their natal charts indicated.

CHAPTER IX

Employer or Employee?

Some natives can only be happy and fulfill their manifest destiny if they are at the head of their own enterprise. Others almost shudder with horror at the bare idea. The responsibility appals them. Here again it is a matter of the horoscope.

To determine leadership qualities is almost elementary. A preponderance or otherwise of planets or angles in cardinal signs shows at a glance if this is present or subordinate. Planets in cardinal signs indicate a leadership which goes deeper than that shown by cardinal signs on the angles. The latter is more showy but less effective. If fixed sign planets and angles are below average, the need of a partner is indicated to supply the deficiency. The partner should be strong in this direction. However, if the partnership house is bad, the native might work the situation out through the agency of a competent manager long on fixed signs.

Without cardinal signs a native may still be successful in his own business or profession if fixed signs are powerful. He will do best in that case by delegating the figurehead leadership to someone else, preferably someone strong in the cardinal region, while he remains the power behind the throne. This role is frequently assumed by ♏ and ♌—less often by ♒ and ♉.

Thus Mussolini, who has permitted Victor Emanuel to remain titular head of the Italian Kingdom and is

said even to show the latter every mark of deference
and respect, actually rules Italy, with the King a mere
figurehead. Mussolini has ☉ in ♌ with ♏ rising. ☽ is
in a common sign, ♊.

On the other hand nobody rules in Germany except
Hitler (as this is written). The fuehrer of the Third
Reich has a cardinal sign, ♎, rising; ☽ is also cardinal
in ♑, while ☉ is fixed in ♉. Hitler has the horoscope
of a born leader—4 planets, 2 angles cardinal; 4 planets,
2 angles fixed; only 2 planets common. It is no endorse-
ment of his character or policies to point this out.

Mussolini, strange as it may seem, does not have the
horoscope of a leader. He has only two planets and no
angles in cardinal signs and neither of these planets are
his rulers. His fixed signs are above the average, with
3 planets (including his ruler ☉, and ☿ the mind planet),
also 2 angles, one of them his Ascendant. Common
signs, however, are over-emphasized with 5 planets and
two angles. The abject failure, at least up to the middle
of January, 1941 when this is written, of his campaigns
against both Britain and Greece which he is said to
have planned himself, bear out the horoscopic evidence
of lack of true leadership. Against poor weak Ethiopia
he could prevail by sheer numbers and superior equipment. Confronted by the determined Greeks and British
with as good and better than anything he could produce,
his deficiency in resource was quickly betrayed. There
have been few military failures in modern history so
pronounced as that of the boastful Il Duce, whose title
has turned out to be a pitiful misnomer.*

* Since this was written, Mussolini appears to have fallen completely
under the domination of Hitler.

Common sign natives are not barred from the professions or from small "one-man" enterprises. They are obviously unsuited, however, for handling masses of employees. The common sign nativity often makes a most likeable person who gets along well with everyone. Such an individual, however, does not possess the "drive" necessary to get the work out of his help. He is unfitted to assume great responsibilities, unequal to making important decisions, and lacks organizing ability. He may be excellent in carrying out details delegated to him by others, but if he in turn must redelegate some of the work to third parties and make himself responsible for their faithful performance, he is likely to be found wanting.

The common sign native is not likely to grieve himself about this state of affairs. Because common signs are preponderant in his chart he has little desire to "boss people about." His ambitions, while they may include wealth and position, do not embrace any desire for the domination of others.

As there are 14 constitutional factors in the natal chart (10 planets, 4 angles) and 3 divisions by constitution (cardinal, fixed, common), the average for each constitution must be 4.67 factors. Thus 4 would be somewhat below and 5 slightly above the average. This is a somewhat misleading method of gauging the relative strength of a constitution, however. There are several other considerations to be taken into account. Thus if only 4 factors were present in a given constitution, if one of these was ⊙, the importance of this luminary is such that he may be reckoned as the equivalent of at least two other planets. The Ascendant is the

most important of angles and may likewise be accounted
as equal to two planets. ☽ is worth, by rule-of-thumb,
perhaps one and one-half—in a female horoscope almost
as much as ☉. The ruler of the Ascendant or Sun-sign,
or any planet exactly on or nearly on the Ascendant
should equal in value almost any two others. ☿, which
rules the mind, is worth more than ordinary planets.

We thus see that Mussolini's fixed constitution with
☉ (which is also his principal ruler) there and his
Ascendant there, besides ☿, is much stronger than the
mere slight numerical preponderance would convey.
Yet his two subordinate rulers, ♂ and ♇, are both in
common signs, while the cardinal quadruplicity contains only the obscure ♃ and ♀. Yet ♃ is exalted in ♋
which gives it rather more than average significance but
still leaves the leadership signs wholly undistinguished.

The fact that Mussolini, a very great world figure,
has an inferior leadership horoscope yet holds in the
hollow of his hand the destinies of millions of people,
many of them with much superior leadership horoscopes
to his own, should not be misunderstood.

The natal horoscope is always a relative thing.

Certain substitutes for a preponderance of cardinal
signs may supply leadership qualities to some extent,
providing planets or angles in the cardinal group are not
wholly lacking. Thus many planets in angular houses
("Accidentally Dignified," is the terminology for planets
so placed) will give a certain love of the limelight which
will tend to thrust the native forward. Of themselves,
however, accidentally dignified planets are by no means
the equivalent in leadership of cardinal signs. They do,
however, bring opportunities for the assumption of re-

sponsibility into the life, and with two or three reasonably strong planets cardinal, the native may still enjoy
a certain prominence in his circle. Accidentally dignified
planets minus cardinal signs may bring the opportunities but the native is little likely to avail himself of
them.

A strong planet on the Ascendant (☉, ♅, ♄ or ♂)
may be taken as of about equal strength to one in a
cardinal sign—perhaps rather stronger. But it should
be within 5° of orb of the rising degree. It is just as
strong in the twelfth as in the first, providing it is within
5° of the Ascendant. President Franklin D. Roosevelt
has ♅ in the first house within about 3° of the Ascendant. He is short on cardinal signs, having only 1 planet
(the Moon) posited therein. He is tremendously long
on fixed signs, no fewer than 7 planets being in this constitution. No one can deny that Mr. Roosevelt is a man
of iron will, yet his leadership is rather unobtrusive and
he is said to listen intently to advice before making
up his mind. This example is cited without its being
intended either to commend or condemn Mr. Roosevelt's politics. Your overwhelmingly cardinal leader
seldom consults anyone but relies wholly on his own
judgment. If the horoscope is otherwise good he may
rise to great heights by this self-complacency. If on the
afflicted side, however, it will certainly bring him to
grief.

Never hesitate to follow the indications of the cardinal-
fixed-common groupings in determining whether to play
a lone hand, to strive for achievement within the framework of some large organization or to embark on the
struggle for topflight recognition as a leader and director

of others. A letter received recently by the author from a lady in California whose son (personally unknown to him) he advised by all means to get into business for himself rather than remain in the employ of others, well illustrates the good that can be done by this method. It reads:

"I especially want to thank you for something. Some time ago you advised us, through my son's horoscope, he would be more successful as owner of his own business than as an employee. At the time could not see our way clear, but worked on it. A year ago succeeded, and he finds himself so much happier that my heart is filled with gratitude to you. Thanks a million. Long life to you and much success."

NOTE: The references to Hitler, Mussolini and Franklin Roosevelt have been left in as although these three personages have long since vanished from the scene, their careers and personalities are so well known that they still serve as appropriate examples.

CHAPTER X

Partners

W<small>HILE</small> it is a traditional rule in astrology that natives of opposite signs are well adapted to each other matrimonially, this is by no means the case with a business or professional partnership. Those with opposite signs rising or ⊙ in opposing signs are not unlikely to be mutually antipathetic. However the harmony or otherwise of the two horoscopes concerned is the deciding factor.

Partnership should not be undertaken unless a preponderance of seventh house factors in the natal horoscope are good. There should be a clear preponderance, not merely a surplusage of one or two factors on the favorable side. Count the favorable and unfavorable aspects, the exaltations, dignities, detriments and falls, counting the two former favorable and the two latter unfavorable. This is as good a rule of thumb as any, and rule of thumb will suffice here because only one question is to be decided: Is partnership desirable or undesirable? Rules 21, 22, 23 and 24 in Chapter II should be followed to ascertain the factors involved.

If the answer is negative the native should dismiss the idea of partnership. But as this may be more easily said than done, due to conditions not within his control, suggestions will be given for mitigating a bad partnership horoscope by at least taking advantage of as many astrological offsets as possible.

The most important is the finding of a partner with a horoscope harmonious to the native's own. Uncanny as it may seem, this is far more likely to be found by a native with a good partnership horoscope than with a poor one. Some mysterious principle of attraction seems to draw the right co-worker to the possessor of a first class set of seventh house factors, and the wrong one to a native with a poor partnership rating. Under very favorable directions (progressions, etc.) the latter may, however, discover a partner as nearly suited to his own personality as the best factors in his horoscope permit. In any case partnership should be entered into under directions which favor it.

It is true there is an old astrological adage to the effect that one cannot get more out of the horoscopic bag than there is in it. In other words that the possibilities are always conditioned by the natal chart, no matter how good the current directions may be. Under wholly good directions, however, the best of the natal aspects of a similar nature are galvanized into activity, while those of a contrary type are held in abeyance. It is therefore possible to "defeat" an adverse seventh house, if it is not too bad, under good influences by direction, providing there is some leverage natally on the good side for the directional influences to take hold of.

It is assumed that the reader knows how to direct (or progress, as it is sometimes rather inaccurately termed) a horoscope. It must be insisted, however, that to take one type of direction and ignore all the rest as is sometimes done, is worse than useless as an entirely wrong picture may be drawn. In his own work the author takes the following current influences, lists them all under Favorable and Unfavorable heads and then casts a balance sheet:

1. Progressed ☉.
2. Progressed ☽.
3. Progressed MC.
4. Progressed Asc.
5. ☉ by 7-year cycle. (☉ moving from its natal place at the rate of one sign every 7 years or $4^2/7°$ per year. Figure from birthdate).
6. Solar Eclipse. (Taking all aspects made by the Eclipse to positions in the natal chart within an orb of 5°. Conjunctions are usually bad unless both ☉ and ☽ are in natal good aspect to the conjoined planets). A Solar Eclipse, in the author's opinion, has influence until the next Solar Eclipse and is strongest about half-way.
7. Transits of the major planets, ♇, ♆, ♅, ♄ and ♃.
8. Transits by parallel of the major planets. (Orb of only 1° each way).

Except where otherwise noted an orb of 1½° either way should be allowed. All directions are to natal positions only.

There are other types of direction but the above are the most important.

In considering the net effect on the question of partnership of the prevailing aspects especial attention should be paid to:

(a) Aspects to natal planets in the seventh house. If to more than one, that planet nearest the cusp is the most important.

(b) Aspects to the planet ruling the sign on the cusp of the seventh.

(c) Aspects to ♀, normal seventh house ruler.

(d) Aspects to planet ruling any sign intercepted in seventh.

Preference over all of the above should be given to any progressed or transiting planet or eclipse actually falling in the seventh house itself, especially if within 5° of the cusp. Such planet, if in conjunction with a natal seventh house planet, would be of extraordinary significance.

In estimating the power of the current directions take those involving seventh house factors as listed above, into principal account. Those not directly concerned should not be wholly ignored, but are coöperative only. If a majority of all partnership factors are favorable at a given time, even though numerically more bad directions than good are prevailing, partnership might still be undertaken. It is better, of course, in any enterprise, to select a time when there is a heavy general preponderance of good directions over bad. Lengthy periods sometimes elapse, however, when this does not occur. Often it is not possible to avoid certain kinds of specialized activity because the current influences are unfavorable to it. In that case there is always a minor cycle within the major cycle, even on a given day, when the "local" or temporary aspects are such as to mitigate the adverse nature of the prevailing major influences. Such periods are determined by *transits* of ☉, ☽, Asc. and MC. (♂, ♀ and ☿ may also be considered but are minor in effect and if the first four mentioned are favorable may be ignored).

The technique of mitigation of unfavorable major directions seems to have been used with telling effect by Hitler in calculating the best periods for initiation of his various political and warlike moves. There is, of course, a limit to the possibility of a native neutralizing a bad natal or progressed horoscope by this means, but a long series of at least secondary successes may be obtained by taking advantage of the fleeting few moments which are constantly presenting themselves as "ideal" for the start of some given undertaking. The baffling ability of the Nazi fuehrer to outguess and outmaneuver his opponents in the early stages of the war is (astrologically) to be laid to his skilful manipulation of the daily aspects to his own horoscope. Yet when thwarted by the stubborn British who, unconscious of the astrological verities involved, of course, refused to let him take the initiative at the time and place he desired, his ever menacing background of major bad aspects asserted itself and he found himself held in check. At this writing the ultimate outcome is in doubt. It would not be, in the opinion of this writer, if the British knew and used astrology as their formidable opponent knows and uses it.

In comparing the horoscopes of the two prospective partners, certain harmonies (or the reverse) are of supreme importance. Everything else is subordinate, though where these major factors are not present, the matter has to be decided by such other comparisons as exist.

The "Number One" indications of a successful business association are:

(1) ☉ in one natal chart in place of ☽ in the other.

(2) ♃ in one conjunction ☉, ☽, Asc. or MC. in the other.

(3) ♃ in one conjunction any planet in seventh or ruling seventh in the other.

(4) ♀ in one conjunction the points listed in (2) and (3).

In horoscope comparisons, aspects from a planet in one chart to a planet or point in the other are not nearly so important as the conjunctions.

Conjunctions and aspects should be exact within 1° either way. Regular natal orbs of planets do not apply in comparison horoscopes.

Principal inharmonious comparisons are:

(a) ♄ or ♂ in one chart on any important point in the other, as ☉, ☽, Asc., MC., ruler, or ruler of seventh.

(b) ♄ or ♂ on any planet in seventh or tenth.

If only minor comparisons, good or bad, can be made, indications of any striking success is not great. There may be reasonable harmony but this is obviously not the prime motive behind a business partnership. Only in a natal chart brilliantly favorable to partnership, should a joint venture be undertaken with one whose comparisons are indifferent.

Many promising business projects come to grief because the wrong people (astrologically speaking) are associated in them. The simple method of comparing horoscopes which can be exhaustively done in an hour or two, may save years of incompatibility or downright antagonism between two people Nature never intended should enter into a business partnership with each other. The technique is not beyond the capability of even a beginner, providing he knows how to set up a chart accurately and observes care in making his comparisons. It is very much worth while, where partnership is contemplated.

The actual moment at which a partnership is entered into is the completion of the signing of the partnership papers. If the partnership is informal, without any written agreement, then the exact moment one or other of the partners opens the door of the new establishment for business. If the business is already a going concern, then the moment the new partner enters the premises to take up his duties. Intent is everything in astrology as in law. Whenever the intent to consummate the partnership is definitely indicated by both parties, that is the moment the relationship has been entered into.

CHAPTER XI

The Right Time to Start

THE Wisdom that "mightily and sweetly ordereth all things" seems insistent upon the observance of its natural laws regarding time. We ignore them at our peril. The ancient scriptural writer enunciated this great truth in succinct language (Ecclesiastes III: 1–8):

"To every thing there is a season, and a time to every purpose under the heaven: A time to be born, and a time to die; a time to plant and a time to pluck up that which is planted; a time to kill and a time to heal; a time to break down and a time to build up . . . a time to get and a time to lose; a time to keep and a time to cast away."

He might have added: "A time to go into business and a time to refrain from going into business; a time to look for a position and a time not to look."

In the last chapter (Partners) the technique of judging by the current directions the advisability or otherwise of selecting a partner at any particular period was given. The same technique differently applied governs the most desirable time to go into business, to hang up one's shingle in a profession or to apply for a position.

The most promising directions for the latter are the following:

(1) Good aspects to any planet in the sixth house.

(2) Same to the ruler of the sixth.

(3) Same to ☿, normal ruler of the sixth.

(4) Same to planets in the second, to ruler of the second or to ♀, normal ruler of the second.

(5) General good aspects, which are coöperative only, especially those affecting the ruler or rulers of the type of occupation selected.

For the start of a business or profession:

(1) Good aspects to any planet in the tenth house.

(2) Good aspects to the MC.

(3) Good aspects to ruler of MC.

(4) Same to ♄, normal tenth house ruler.

(5) Same to planets in the second, to ruler of the second or to ♀, normal ruler of the second.

(6) General good aspects, especially to the planets ruling occupation selected.

NOTE: Progressions of the MC. are particularly potent.

As with partnership, so intent governs the actual start of a business enterprise. Any symbolical act, as the opening of the doors of a store for business, marks the start of the project. But the act must not be far-fetched, merely to take advantage of a favorable time. The influences fasten themselves on an actual not a hypothetical birth, whether of an infant child or an infant business. The moment the child starts to lead a life independent of its mother is the moment of birth. Usually, but not always, this is the instant of the severing of the umbilical cord. The author knows of a case where the child was born with the cord wrapped around its throat, apparently strangled. It took half-an-hour to start breathing. The natal horoscope for the moment of delivery bore no relation to the appearance or disposition of the native—was in fact an astrological impossibility as applied to him. A horoscope set for the exact moment breathing started represented this native perfectly. The case is known to be authentic, details being furnished by the child's father, a prominent physician, who was present and assisted in starting the breathing.

Similarly, the moment the business or professional venture is launched is its birthtime, and the aspects then prevailing, as applied to the chart of the native concerned, marks the influences which govern. A secondary horoscope—that of the business or profession itself—may be set up in the same way as a regular birth horoscope of an individual. A good deal of information regarding the ups and downs of the venture as such may be gleaned in this way, but the important thing to consider is the relationship of the native's directions, prevailing at that exact moment, to his own natal horoscope.

By way of guidance in determining the birth moment of a new enterprise a few suggestions may be given. Reference was made above to symbolical acts. Thus the driving of a golden spike into the final connecting rail used to mark the completion of a railroad. The last hammer tap by the celebrity officiating at the ceremony would signal the birth of that particular line. Any final words spoken in the dedicating of a building would be of similar import with preference given to the actual statement, "I dedicate this building to . . ."

A young lawyer or doctor taking his seat at his desk for the first time, with intent to start practicing, would mark the commencement of his career, rather than the mere opening of his doors.

Alan Leo considers that the sale of the first number

of a new periodical is the birth moment of the publication, and because of the eminence of this authority his view is entitled to respect.

In opening a store, however, where business hours are fixed, there seems no doubt that the exact start of the first business day would mark the birth moment. Thus if the store opened at 9 A.M., the fact that the first customer did not appear until 9:15 would be irrelevant. 9 A.M. would be the birthtime.

The exact moment of the filing of incorporation papers as recorded by the State, marks the official birth of a Corporation as such. This is of great importance in selecting investments. The subject is foreign to the purpose of the present work but it may be said in passing that the astrological harmonies or disharmonies exist, not only between the horoscopes of individuals but between the horoscopes of corporate entities and individuals. If the malefic ♄ appear in the Corporation chart in the same degree as for instance ☉, ☽ or ♀ in the investor's natal horoscope, in the absence of powerful offsets from ♃ or other planets it is unlikely that the latter will realize much profit from his investment. This, however, is a different branch of astrology and cannot be dealt with here.

If a prospective employee can somehow obtain at least the birthdate of his employer-to-be, and compare planetary positions in his own and the employer's chart, as closely as may be without the birthtime, this has considerable value. The technique of comparison is as outlined in Chapter X (Partners), with certain modifications. Partners are presumably business equals but as between employer and employee a different relationship exists. Thus ⊙ in former's chart in opposition or square to ♀ in the latter's would have a tendency to overawe the employee and prevent him from obtaining full recompense for his work (⊙ = authority; ♀ = money). ⊙ ♂, or P ♀ would be favorable but employer's ♂ over employee's ruler would denote oppression and irritability from the former.

The most valuable horoscope for comparison is that of the immediate superior with whom the employee will mostly come in contact. This will give day-to-day relationships, always very important for peace of mind and early advancement. The natal chart of the owner of the business or of the Corporation is, however, the long range factor for success or failure, astrologically speaking.

Needless to say, no cross aspects however favorable will take the place of hard and intelligent work, loyalty, and the right kind of ambition. The native must do his part, but his work may be rendered much easier and his path to promotion greatly smoothed if the comparative horoscopes are harmonious.

Should they be adverse he can still win his way through, but at the price of expending considerable unnecessary energy which could be better employed in other ways.

CHAPTER XII

The Time to Apply for a Position

IT CAN hardly have escaped the notice of any ordinarily observant person that business interviews sometimes proceed with amazing smoothness, each party thereto saying and doing just the right thing to help matters along to a satisfactory conclusion. At other times the interview may go very well for one of the parties, not so well for the others. Still again it may go badly for all and break up with nothing accomplished.

Astrologers claim that the underlying reasons for these outcomes are the planetary and sidereal influences prevailing *at the beginning* of the interview. The influences referred to are those prevailing in relation to the natal horoscope of the individual initiating the interview. Current transits of ⊙, ☽ and planets to each other, so beloved of the daily newspaper horoscopes, are a factor so minor they need hardly be taken into account at all. It is quite true that if the daily aspects are mainly harmonious they will contribute a modicum of help to the native's own harmonious aspects. But the former may be quite adverse—even definitely antagonistic to the enterprise in hand—and if they are in favorable positions to key points in the native's own chart, he can still register entirely satisfactory results from his efforts.

It is easily demonstrable, for instance, that on a day declared to be "excellent to apply for a position," thousands will apply for positions and be turned down. It is a great deal more trouble to apply current transits to each individual's own horoscope than to write a general prescription applicable to all the earth's millions. But it represents the difference between the automatic action (if any) of a cheap patent medicine and the painstaking diagnosis and treatment of an outstanding medical specialist.

The informed astrologer never ceases to cry out against the "boiler-plate horoscope," that astrological monstrosity which seemingly has learned only of the months and knows nothing of years, days, hours or minutes. Anybody born when ☉ is in ♈ or ♉ or what-not has the same appearance, character and fate. Similarly the transits prevailing each day affect the whole of creation alike. These horoscopic cure-alls have brought real astrology, most painstaking of sciences, into understandable disrepute among those who from ignorance regard them as representative of the ancient Science of the Stars. But no one is more bitterly contemptuous of this degradation of one of the grandest arts known to man, than is the competent practitioner of astrology. The difference is that between the AstrologER (the correct term) and the "AstroloGIST" (a popular word having no dictionary sanction). The latter term may well be used to include the astrological charlatans, the extent of whose knowledge appears to end with the ability to recite the verse beginning, "Thirty days hath September."

The native looking for a position should therefore pay no attention whatever to newspaper or magazine advice assuring him that "this is a good day to secure a job." To know if it is really a good day and exactly what period of a "good day" is best, he must compare the transiting ☉ and ☽ with his own natal positions and then, having arrived at a satisfactory hour, narrow it down to an exact minute by transiting MidHeaven and Ascendant positions.

Reference should be made to Chapters X and XI where the method for determining the current major influences is given. These always constitute the main "atmosphere" prevailing, and nothing can be done about them if they are adverse except to wait until they have disappeared. This may involve a delay of months, or even years, so that in most of the affairs of life it is quite impracticable to defer action until they are wholly or largely good. They set the bounds, so to say, of the possibilities open to the native at a given time of success or failure, but they do not ordain either success or failure. Within this major framework all kinds of constructive effort may take place. It is only the *scale* of the success which is determined by the major directions. Success may be very great when these are mainly favorable. But small, relative successes are possible even when the progressions are largely adverse. As noted in a previous chapter, this appears to be Hitler's method. He tries to catch the "Grade A" major periods whenever they are available. But if events force him to move under "Grade B" or "Grade C" major influences he takes care to select only "Grade A" minor influences for the inception of his warlike projects. And this he (or anyone else) can readily do because, while the major movements of planets and angles extend over years and months, the minor movements of some of them cover only weeks, days, hours and even minutes.

For huge advances we need the aid of the most important favorable directions to key points in our natal charts. Blessed is he who can start a business, apply for a job or ask for a raise in salary, when the progressed ☽ trines his natal ☉. And particularly if ☉ is in good aspect to ☽ in his birth horoscope. But that particular progression comes only once in 14 years and lasts about 3 months. A sextile (not quite so good but still helpful) of progressed ☽ to ☉ occurs at varying intervals twice in 28 years. Obviously one can hardly plan one's future in detail based on aspects so very infrequent.

Yet it is not impossible to plan at long range to take full advantage of any unusual aggregation of good progressions falling over a given period. These may be figured out a lifetime in advance if desired and the native may build his future on a sound astrological basis by directing his efforts so that they may, so far as possible, culminate during one of the highly favorable periods. This is not quite so difficult as may appear. The aspects themselves will automatically mould existing circumstances so that they tend to bring their greatest good into the life at the zenith of the favoring period. Yet by working with them, with eyes open to the manner in which their influences are operating, incomparably greater results are procurable. The old adage, "Nature unaided fails," though not entirely applicable to the progressed horoscope, is true in a measure. The tide, "taken at its flood" may wash us in to shore, but we shall get there far more speedily and efficiently if we do a little rowing on our own hook.

Letting the major directional framework, therefore, come "as is," seeing that we cannot do otherwise without perhaps waiting an indefinite length of time, we should select a day to apply for our new job when ☽ transits ✶ or △.

(a) A planet in the sixth house of the natal horoscope, providing such planet is not in bad aspect to ☽ natally (if good, so much the better), and providing it has more good aspects than bad. Also providing that it is not afflicted with more bad aspects than it has good by progression.

(b) If no planet possesses these qualifications then take planet which rules sign on cusp of sixth house, subject to same qualifications and conditions.

(c) If this too is not available, take ☿, normal ruler of sixth house and therefore of employment. Same conditions applicable.

(d) If ☿ has to be passed up for like reasons, take any good planet in ♍. Same conditions.

(e) If none of previous four suggestions can be carried out try a planet in tenth house or ruling tenth house, or take MidHeaven itself. Observe same conditions on all these alternatives.

(f) If there is still failure to find the ideal planet, the second house occupants may be similarly experimented with, second house ruler or ♀.

(g) ☉, ☽ or ruler of Ascendant are about the last chances. It is most unlikely, however, that the native will not find some planet possessing the needed requirements and without drawbacks, before he has gone this far down on the list.

Having selected the planet, ascertain within which

hours the transiting ☽ makes a ✳ or △ aspect to it. Allow an orb of 1½° each way. The aspect is stronger when separating than when forming. As ☽ moves from a little less than 12° to a little more than 15° per day such aspect will last from 5 to 6 hours, being exact at its midmost point. The 1½° orb is more or less approximate and it will be safe to allow 6 hours in all cases, even when ☽ is moving at its fastest.

Make sure that ☉ is not making an adverse transit to the planet selected or this is likely to frustrate the good effect of ☽. Also be sure that while it transits ✳ or △ your good planet, ☽ does not make a □ or ☍ to some other planet in your natal chart or a ☌ to a malefic (♇, ♆, ♅, ♄) or to ☋. However if ☽ is natally in good aspect to any of the four malefics, its ☌ by transit will not hurt, but watch out for the ☌ ☋ and for all □'s and ☍'s.

Having steered clear of all these, we next narrow down the time to within a minute or two by taking the transiting MidHeaven and Ascendant. This is done by the same method as in setting up a natal horoscope. From the ephemeris note down the Sidereal Time for noon of the selected day. From the table of houses for the place in which the native is living (*not* the birthplace, if this is somewhere else), choose a Sidereal Time which falls within the favorable transiting period of ☽ to the planet you have decided upon. Give preference to the latter rather than the earlier half of the period. Remember that the Sidereal Time at noon bears the same relation to the Sidereal Times listed in the table of houses as 12 noon bears to any time on the clock. Thus on June 22nd, 1941 the Sidereal Time at Noon is 6–1–6. If the native resides in New York we add the customary 50 seconds for the 5 hours difference between New York and Greenwich (England) time. Whatever the difference this must be added (or subtracted in Eastern longitudes). Be careful of the astrologer's latest pitfall, Daylight Saving Time. Make the necessary 1 hour correction or your calculations will be worthless. Then if you desire to know what the Sidereal Time will be at 3 P.M., June 22nd, 1941, merely add 3 hours plus 50 seconds, plus 30 seconds (the 10 seconds per hour sidereal correction for the 3 hours elapsed since noon) and you have 3 hours, 1 minute, 20 seconds to add to the Sidereal Time at noon. Thus:

$$
\begin{array}{r}
6 - 1 - 6 \\
50 \\
3 - 0 - 0 \\
30 \\
\hline
9 - 2 - 26
\end{array}
$$

Now refer to your Table of Houses for New York and take the closest Sidereal Time you can find to 9–2–26. This proves to be 9–1–53, at which moment the MidHeaven is in 13° ♌ and the Ascendant in 5° ♏ 53. There will be a slight correction for the 33″ difference, but to all intents and purpose we may say 6° ♏ are rising and 13° ♌ on the MidHeaven. This might or might not be what we wanted. Let us take a concrete instance.

Supposing the planet we had selected was ♃ in 8° ♒, and we had picked on June 22nd because on the afternoon of that date ☽ would transit in △ that degree. As a matter of fact June 22nd, 1941 falls on Sunday, so unless we could see our future employer at his home or, by some special dispensation, get a Sunday interview at his office, we would have to pass up that day in favor of some other. This is of no consequence, however, as we are only using the day to illustrate the method.

We find that ☉ in about 1° ♋ makes no adverse transit to anything natal and in fact is ⚹ ☿ in 0° ♉. So far so good. If we could get a good MidHeaven or Ascendant aspect to ♃, our selected planet, that would be ideal. However the range the ☽ transit △ ♃ allows us is only from about 6½° ♊ to 9½° ♊, which journey is covered from about 10 A.M. to 4 P.M. As Sidereal Time at noon is 6–1–6, Sidereal Time at 10 A.M. would be approximately 4–0–0 (allowing for small time corrections) at 10 A.M. and 10–0–0 at 4 P.M. At 4–24–55 Sidereal Time, MidHeaven is in 8° ♊ and Ascendant in 11° ♍ 10. This would give us a clock time of 10:25 A.M. and is the only good MidHeaven aspect available during the chosen period. If Ascendant in 11° ♍ 10 is in no bad aspect to anything natal, this time immediately becomes a possibility, assuming that we can arrange for an interview then. If Ascendant does cast a bad aspect we have to abandon the MidHeaven and see if we can get a good aspect of the Ascendant. Between 4–0–0 and 10–0–0 Sidereal Time, Ascendant moves from about 6° ♍ 12 to 17° ♏ 15. Obviously the only trine it could cast to ♃ in 8° ♒ is from 8° ♎ which it reaches at about 6–42–0 Sidereal Time. This is approximately 12:42 P.M. Sun Time. (Don't forget to correct to Clock Time and to allow for Daylight Saving Time, if in effect). MidHeaven at that moment is in 10° ♋. If we find MidHeaven casts no bad aspect to any natal point we then have our second possibility.

If a bad aspect is cast in either case we have to do our work again, selecting a second choice planet for our MidHeaven or Ascendant aspect—perhaps a third or a fourth choice. If we cannot get either of these angles to throw a favoring ray to the planet to which ☽ has its good aspect (and it is not often possible) then we take as good a substitute as the horoscope affords. If we can arrange so that MidHeaven throws a △ or ✳ to one planet and Ascendant to another, that is fine, and with our good ☽ transit we may feel we have done as well as possible and proceed to arrange for our interview with the confidence that only one versed in the astrological laws can know, when he has taken full precautions to select the most auspicious time.

CHAPTER XIII

The Interview

OBJECTIONS invariably present themselves to students of vocational astrology who hear for the first time of the importance of beginning an interview regarding a position at a given minute. "How in the world can that be done?" is their unspoken inquiry. How can one be certain that the prospective employer will make an appointment for the time indicated as being best for the applicant? If he can be induced to make it for that time, how can there be any assurance that he will not be tied up with something else and keep the applicant waiting until the auspicious moment has passed? Also what constitutes the beginning of an interview—the exact time the applicant appears at the employer's place of business—when he is admitted to the presence of the employer—or when the conversation begins?

Attention will be given to all these points and it may be said at the outset that in practice these difficulties turn out to be far less than in theory. The author of this book (who is also in a prosaic wholesale business having nothing to do with astrology) has found it perfectly possible to arrange affairs so that important business interviews were started at exactly the moment he desired. Occasionally, but not very often, circumstances frustrated this but if the matter to be discussed was of sufficient importance an excuse for deferring its consideration could usually be presented and a later time set, already figured out for just such a contingency. As a matter of fact all should not be staked on one time—the native should have several satisfactory periods already chosen. It is not more difficult to alter a suggested appointment for astrological reasons than it is to change it for ordinary physical ones. The other person need not be given the real reason or any reason for that matter. The time suggested is simply not convenient and the native counters with a suggestion of his own—or another and another, if need be.

It is true we cannot well "play horse" with a prospective employer, who usually reserves the right to set the time for the interview and will make short work of the applicant if the latter starts boggling about it. However, such difficulties are not insurmountable. If the application is made by letter (which also should be started and mailed under "right" aspects), a time or several times may be diplomatically suggested. If the employer chooses one of these the native should be on hand well ahead of time. Some employers seem to feel it absolutely necessary to keep an applicant sitting on a bench in an ante-room for half-an-hour or so before they will deign to see him.

But assuming this hurdle has been surmounted and the applicant is sitting across from the great man's desk ready to be interviewed, how can one insure that at exactly the right minute and second, the interview will begin?

Well, fortunately Nature is not quite so exacting as that. It does not have to be at exactly a given minute or second. The MidHeaven and Ascendant remain approximately on the same degree for about 4 minutes.

And as there is an "orb" of about a degree and a half either way, that gives a further latitude of approximately 12 minutes more (6 minutes each way from the exact moment). Thus a total "possible" period of 16 minutes is available and with a little *finesse* on the applicant's part he should be able to direct the conversation into the proper channel within this time range. He should however try to delay it until *after* the culminating minute rather than to have it commence before. As previously stated, separating aspects are stronger than those just forming which is fortunate, as it is usually easier to delay a business conversation than to start it prematurely. There are always other things to talk about, even to a prospective employer, than the immediate business in hand and—here is the point to bear in mind—the interview begins at the exact moment the native (not the employer) either broaches the subject which has brought him there or answers the interviewer's first question. However, the native should take the initiative in order to come fully under the sway of the astrological influences he has selected. It is *his* planetary party, so to speak, and he loses something of the full effect of the aspects if the other person starts the ball rolling.

Merely to announce his name does not mark the "birth" of the interview, unless at the same time he states his business. But if he says, "I am John Smith. You wrote me to come in about a position," the die is cast and the interview has begun at whatever time he uttered the last nine words of the sentence. If he glances at his watch as he enters the "presence," and finds he needs to stall for a few minutes before the desired time arrives, this should not be too difficult. A remark about the weather, the size of the building or almost any casual thing which occurs to him may hold the fort for the opportune moment. It is, of course, rather more difficult to create chit-chat when one is applying for a job than if the meeting concerns some other business matter, but with a little intelligent handling of the situation it is by no means impossible.

The question may arise, will the prospective employer resent this loquacity on the part of one applying for a job? That, of course, depends upon how it is done. If the native doubts his own ability in this direction he might try getting the employer to do the talking. There is a danger here, however; the latter may talk past the fateful moment or he may switch to the subject in hand too soon. With the 16 minute leeway there should not be much hazard here. The native's worst peril is that the phone may ring and the employer be tied up in a lengthy conversation.

But it must not be forgotten that within this entire 16 minute period, the native's current aspects are good —exceptionally good, in fact, otherwise he would not have selected that particular time. Unlucky "breaks" such as the above are therefore really not due to happen and probably will not happen. At least that has been the author's experience, and he has used these "selected times" in his own business and advised others regarding their use, for years. If the temporary aspects are good and the major framework not too bad, things move along like a charm. Everything goes as hoped. The other person says just the right thing—you say just the right thing. When you leave you have no regrets—no looking back to think, "Why did I say that? Why didn't I say this? What a bad slip I made there! Why did I pass up that marvellous opening he gave me?" and so on.

An excellent example of how almost unbelievably perfect results may be obtained in face of the most unpromising circumstances may here be given, as it is in the author's own experience of only a few months ago. It does not concern an interview for a position but something even more vital—the shutting off of supplies needed to carry on a business, because of shortages caused by defense priorities. With dwindling stocks available the writer decided to make a 600 mile trip and plead his case with the source of supply in the hope of being tided through the emergency. As several hundred other buyers all had the same idea at about the same time and there was nothing like enough to go around, the situation was pretty desperate. It was made more so when the concern in question, upon learning of the proposed visit, first sent a special delivery letter, then a telegram and finally made a long distance call urging the writer not to come. The tenor of all the communications was the same: "You are wasting your time. We can do nothing for you."

The writer, who has his fair share of fixed signs besides an abiding faith in the efficacy of a properly selected astrological time, ignored the warnings and went anyway. But first he carefully chose a time when the transiting ☽ was △ ☉, △ natal ☽ and ♂ ♂. All three of these aspects were good because natal ☽ is △ ♂ natally. It is also △ ☉ in the natal chart. A better transit could hardly be imagined for the purpose desired. ☉ rules those in position to grant favors. ♂ governs controversies and antagonism. ☽ is part ruler of the particular product on which the shortage exists.

Narrowing down the time by MidHeaven and Ascendant aspects it was possible to obtain at 8:57 Clock Time on the morning of February 19th, 1941 a sextile to the natal Ascendant from the MidHeaven and a trine to natal ♄, the business planet, from the Ascendant. This set up is almost incredibly good, more particularly as the time, about 9 A.M., is the logical one for such an interview.

At 8:57 A.M. on the dot, the writer walked into the office of the official on whom the fate of his business depended and plunged into conversation regarding the shortage. Several hours later he left, having gained everything he requested without a solitary exception. His business associates were surprised beyond measure, but the writer, having from lengthy experience the utmost faith in astrology, was not surprised.

Obviously one's case has to be good or no amount of good aspects will suffice. It is useless to rely on even the best influences to obtain a position for which one is not qualified. But given proper qualifications, the ability to present them in convincing form, and a position available in which they can be used, the clinching factor in this writer's firm belief is the right astrological influence under which to make the bid for the job.

CHAPTER XIV

From the Employer's Side

Every Personnel Director should possess some knowledge of vocational astrology. It would help him immeasurably in placing the right people in the right jobs. Records of previous employment, references, high school and college credits, are all good rule-of-thumb guides but they lack the precision of an astrological analysis of character, talent and ability. It will no doubt seem ridiculous to say it and may provoke scornful laughter, but there should be an astrological division in every Personnel Department. It should be directed by the most competent astrologer procurable, whose own chart should conclusively demonstrate that he has the qualifications for so exacting a position. In a large institution he should be assisted by a suitable staff.

This will be done one day, of course. Certain moving picture producers are known to have their astrological advisers. Hitler is reported on very good authority to have a board of five, besides being a very able astrologer himself. We shall get around to it in course of time as we have got around to so many other reforms in business which once were sneered at as the dreams of idealists and visionaries.

Most employers require an applicant to state his birthdate. Even without the time certain facts of value can be gleaned from the sign positions and aspects of the planets. But with a little knowledge of astrology a very good guess at the rising sign may be made from the personal appearance, mannerisms and interests of the native. Scientific rectification, of course, requires correction also by important events of the life, but even without these a clue can often be obtained which, in light of later information, proves very close to accuracy in the rising sign determined upon.

As each rising sign contains six modifying "faces" (sets of 5° each), slightly differing from each other, a further narrowing down is possible. In the absence of exact information the native may be judged as to rising sign by observing him closely, providing one has a fair working knowledge of the general appearance conferred by each sign.

It must be emphasized that the popular notion that the birth month marks the sign the native is born under, and that his appearance conforms to the Sun sign, is the rankest of astrological heresy. Only if the birth took place around sunrise (when Sun sign and Ascendant are the same) is this generally true. A native might be born with ☉ in ♉ and ♎ rising and look no more like a Taurean than does Hitler, who has that particular combination, which does not mean that many ♉ characteristics are not present, but they form the deeper, rather than the more observable layers of the character.

As a matter of fact, Hitler's face is somewhat more Taurean than would ordinarily be the case with a native who had ☉ in ♉ and ♎ rising, for the reason that in his chart ♀ (ruler of both ♎ and ♉) also appears in ♉ where it is very strong. Besides this, another planet, ♂, is there. None of these aspects the Ascendant in any way and the Ascendant is the prime factor in personal appearance. An aspecting planet, particularly from ☉ sign, will modify it in some degree and if from ☉ sign will give the latter a prominence it might not otherwise possess. A ☉ sign containing three or more planets, however, is always likely to show out a little in the personal appearance even though none of them aspects Ascendant, but it will not usually upset the characteristic expression of the ascending sign.

Thus President Roosevelt has ♍ rising. ☉, ☿ and ♀ are in ♒, making no Ascendant aspect. ♅, ruler of ♒ is almost exactly on the rising degree, bringing out all the characteristics of the powerful ♒ and almost, but not quite, swamping out the rather negative ♍.

Yet the birdlike look which astrologers associate with ♍ is still there, and Mr. Roosevelt's handsome, domed Aquarian head, nevertheless contrives to retain a certain birdlike expression peculiar to ♍. His quick, emphatic movements and his habit of tossing his head in punctuation of his sentences are all very reminiscent of the Mercurial ♍.

In the main, however, it is reasonably safe to sum up the salient sign characteristics of a native by studying him, and mentally classify him as dominated largely by one or other of the 12 great zodiacal signs. This is, of course, assuming that it is not possible to have a proper horoscope cast, which is always the only true scientific method to employ.

With a view to helping personnel directors and employers as well as others to whom such knowledge would be valuable, to size up astrologically those applying to them for positions or with whom they have business dealings in other ways, a brief description is here given of certain striking characteristics each sign confers. The author has, in his own business, hired and trained hundreds of traveling salesmen and sales executives by applying the rules herein given—and has rejected thousands more. Only a brief summary can be given, but the emphasized points have been found to be very peculiar to the particular zodiacal type in each case. Some of the points, so far as is known, are not included in "orthodox" astrological classifications but are based on the writer's own long continued observation.

♈

The nose in this type is nearly always long and rather pointed, with a sort of hump in the middle, sloping down into a valley and then rising slightly again at the end. Eyes unusually piercing. Native quite likely to appear to be staring you out of countenance without any intention of doing so. Adam's apple (in the male) prominent. Manner rather abrupt and impatient. Talk advancement to this type—possibility of his having subordinates of his own to order about (♈ loves this). Will usually respond better to this than to talk of money. Very ambitious and wants to be at the head of something. Fine when he can put over his projects with a rush. Not so good (in absence of fixed signs) when persistence called for.

♉

Look for long lobe of ear, usually present. Hands and feet rather undersized for build. Thick neck. "Bulldog" look. Firm chin. Advancement talk not nearly so appealing to him as talk about money. Has excellent money sense and can usually make it, if not for himself then for others. Not so good as ♈ at originating ideas but better at carrying them out. Bulldog tenacity. Equable temperament when not crossed but a fierce and implacable opponent when aroused.

♊

Almost always tall, thin, rangy. Large hands and feet. Fine, expressive eyes. Often underweight. The "flyer" type. Clever at repartee—a born "wisecracker." Will try to wisecrack his way out of embarrassing situations and quite at a loss if unable to do so, as he often can. Curious about things rather than people. Dexterous with his hands; good mentality but divided energies. Tries to do too much at one time but in his own ♊ field is unexcelled. Not overstrong on system and method but very good improviser.

♋

Broad shoulders, tapering lower limbs. Eyes sometimes appear sleepy but ♋ is quite wideawake. Very sensitive and homeloving. Great respect for tradition and desires to be a "somebody" in the community. Likes to talk about *his* children, *his* home, *his* automobile, *his* hobbies. Bitingly sarcastic when annoyed. Dislikes "scenes." Desires what he thinks is proper respect paid him by those he doesn't know well. A worker until he achieves what he wants, then sometimes becomes insufferably lazy. Tenacious and apparently very sure of himself, but not always able to "take it" if misfortune comes. Reliable worker.

♌

Large nose with spreading nostrils very typical.

Lion-like head with mane of hair (baldness often comes in middle life as with all the fiery signs). Pleasant, open face. Frank manner. Conversation often interlarded with immense amount of unnecessary detail. Very trustworthy. Seldom dishonest. Lover of children and a social "lion." Dignified manner, condescending to subordinates; the ruling rather than the leading type.

♍

Usually rather small features; bottom of face has "pinched in" look, giving resemblance to bird. Very alert in manner. Have trick of following people with their eyes even when sitting down quietly. Curious about people primarily, things secondarily. Finicky about food. Sometimes faddy over health, either using medicines to excess or eschewing them altogether. Best detail workers (♑ second best). Seldom forget any routine duty but dislike to make decisions.

♎

Well modeled features, regular and usually pleasing. Particular about personal appearance. Often part hair in middle. Slender to middle age, then sometimes (but not always) put on flesh. Very good judgment and fine artistic sense. Nearly always have good taste. Humane in their personal contacts though in case of a character such as Hitler (♎ with ♉ ☉) this would not prevent extreme cruelty as a matter of policy.

♏

Strongest sign in the zodiac. Powerful features. Nose curved and large or on the Taurus order but longer.

Ear-lobes often very fleshy. "Penthouse" eyebrows. Formidable appearance. Undaunted fighters with enormous staying power. Can be broken but not bent. Excellent for difficult and dangerous assignments.

$\uparrow$

Equine look. Long face. Teeth usually prominent. $\nearrow$ women have a way of sitting or standing pigeon-toed. The men wind their legs around the chair and appear to be trying to tie them in knots. Very tall; expressive eyes, usually dark. Sometimes Spanish type. Athletic. At their best when full trust is placed in them. Strong religious sense, though not necessarily church-goers.

$\mathcal{V}\mathcal{S}$

Hooked nose and chin. Sometimes flat "goatish" looking face. Usually no ear lobes. Suspicious look. Watery eyes. Scant hair. The "Cassius" type (lean and hungry look). Very capable and hard working. Tremendous respect for the old and established. Dislike innovations. Great worriers. Long lived though constitution not strong and they have many illnesses. Get results by nagging methods, though higher type does it diplomatically. Find fault with most things and are easily irritated, but very staunch when real misfortune befalls. Fine business people. Good executive types but not too easy to get along with.

$\approx$

Good looking, attractive, friendly. Very up-to-date and intelligent. Decisive but carry through without upsetting people. Reliable workers but would rather play. Sense of duty keeps them on the job, and also the necessity of money to gratify their somewhat expensive tastes. Well liked wherever they go and usually envied for something or other. Possess all-round ability and one of the most desirable of the signs.

♓

Fishlike appearance, though often good looking in a rather dreamy way. Small "Cupid's bow" mouth. Small hands and feet. Limbs so short they are almost "fins." Chin close to shoulders with short, thick neck. Prominent eyes. Happy-go-lucky disposition. Philosophical under misfortune which often alternates with amazing good luck. Not seldom end up well-to-do without quite knowing what happened. Lower types addicted to drink, drugs or curious habits. Higher types have great creative imagination, far ahead of their day and generation.

Above are very sketchy outlines intended mainly as an aid to identifying the types. It must not be supposed that all of the pleasant or unpleasant characteristics are present in every person in whom the sign is most prominent. There are a hundred or more factors in each horoscope to be taken into account in appraising character.

It is suggested that the applicant's birthdate be secured (an easy thing to do) and that the rising sign be approximately arrived at by study of the appearance and mannerisms as sketched out above. Such a speculative horoscope is not likely to be accurate but if it is anywhere near so it will give some clue to the native's abilities and the things he is best fitted for.

If an accurate horoscope can be procured the employer has a most reliable guide for placement and advancement of the native in the way most advantageous to both.

CHAPTER XV

Horoscopes of the Successful
(*Foreword*)

IN THE example horoscopes which follow and on which detailed analyses are given, names have been suppressed to avoid embarrassment to the individuals concerned. They have been selected because in each case these natives are happy in their chosen fields and consider themselves successful in what they are doing. They are also regarded as successful by those who know them. In each case the native believes in astrology and admits having received the utmost benefit by following its guidance.

Horoscopes of great national or international figures have purposely not been used for these exhaustive analyses for two reasons. Firstly because the "one in a million" success is of little use as an example to the other 999,999 who aim at only modest success and would perhaps be happier in attaining that than in the fierce limelight which beats about the ultra-successful. Secondly the natal charts of these world figures have been analyzed and super-analyzed *ad nauseam*, and it is the aim of this work, so far as possible, to avoid duplicating existing material. In the brief analyses which follow in a later chapter, some such celebrities have been included, in order to demonstrate striking horoscopic positions or aspects.

The reader is recommended to study these horoscopes and analyses without the feeling that they inevitably indicated that the natives would be successful or would follow these particular lines. They did not. They furnished a background of certain ability, talents, willpower—they also supplied plenty of friction and drawbacks. Others born with closely similar horoscopes may have made greater or less use of the opportunities their astrological equipment provided. The natal chart indicates trends only. The native has great freewill in using or ignoring the sidereal and planetary aids with which he has been provided. True, we can probably always find something in the natal chart which has impelled the individual to follow this or that type of work, even though sheer accident, chance or luck may outwardly seem responsible. But we may, and often do, find some magnificent position or aspect which bears every mark of the ideal occupation for the native, totally ignored or followed only as a hobby or sideline.

Yet the planets do their best. So long as a native is in the wrong occupation everything seems to conspire against his success. In desperation, perhaps, he is forced out of an unpromising career into something which developes amazingly for him and which years later, when he learns something of astrology, he finds was the natural outlet for his talents and energies. Retrograde, but well placed or aspected planets, seem to act in that way. The good they indicate comes into the life after a series of false starts or mediocre success in lines indicated by other planets connected with the occupational houses, but poorly indicated.

Students sometimes express surprise that often there

are many bad aspects as well as good ones in successful
horoscopes. Yet why should there not be? Bad aspects
—squares, oppositions and malefic conjunctions or parallels—bring difficulties, defeats, antagonisms, even
misfortunes. Yet on these hard foundations some of the
most solid edifices of achievement have been erected.
The very good horoscopes—many trines, sextiles,
benefic conjunctions and the like—give great ease of
accomplishment in certain directions, and those directions are by all means to be sought out and followed.
Yet if unleavened by any bad aspects at all, the native
will be almost too successful—and unless the horoscope
indicates a very strong character in other ways, his success may go to his head. He may live life without ever
fully understanding it. Nature must have use for suffer-
ing and adversity—they are so omnipresent in her
works. There is nothing desirable about them in themselves. They are there to be overcome, and in the over-
coming something is added to character and ability
which perhaps could be put there in no other way.

So no one should look at the horoscope of a John D.
Rockefeller or a Henry Ford with the thought, "How
could he help making a success? Look at the natal chart
he has." Many a little business man or bookkeeper may
have a better chart than either of them in certain ways.
But these notables extracted every ounce of the possibilities of their good aspects and used their bad ones to
gain experience. The lesser fry may have as great potentialities, but they will not make the sacrifices their
charts call for, will not think their problems through
intelligently, will not strive mightily to find out what
they are best fitted for. The wonderful guide furnished
by astrology is at the behest of all. Yet it is ignored,

laughed at, treated with contempt by the very people, too often, who need it most.

The student is begged to take astrology seriously. It will be incredible to our enlightened descendants a century hence or less, that we could have committed the folly of allowing such menaces to the human race as Hitler to have a virtual monopoly among the world's rulers, of this greatest of sciences, while those who fought to preserve liberty and civilization turned their backs on it.

It is supposed among the so-called educated to indicate great strength of mind to condemn astrology out of hand, to term it nonsense, to look down one's nose at those who presume to believe in it. Yet which takes the greater strength of character—to follow the lead of the uninformed who parrot the phrase "Astrology is bunk" without the slightest first-hand knowledge—or to proclaim publicly, "I have studied Astrology. I believe in it because I can do no other, without ignoring the evidence of my own senses"?

There are probably many more educated than uneducated people who believe that "there is something in Astrology." Its practitioners boast of a distinguished group of great thinkers including Sir Isaac Newton, the famous astronomers Kepler and Camille Flammarion, and at least one of the Popes. True enough there is a "lunatic fringe" in the astrological movement as in every other. Wild-eyed fanatics make impossible claims, sensational predictions and ridiculous statements they claim are based on the science of the stars. Charlatans exploit popular credulity at profit to themselves. Reputable astrologers regard these fakers as some renowned physician might look on the activities of an advertising quack. They fiercely resent being classified with the dregs of an ancient and honorable profession. One of the best astrological books of recent months is the work of an Oxford M.A. Many astrological writers hold scientific and literary degrees from front rank Universities.

And there is evidence that the Universities themselves will not forever maintain their aloofness to this key science, so badly needed to implement their educational efforts. Some years ago a leading midwestern University invited the author to deliver a lecture on Vocational Astrology and accorded him a respectful and intelligent hearing.

These facts are emphasized because unless the reader is free from preconceived prejudice and will earnestly follow the path his horoscope maps out for his success, he is not doing justice to himself. Yet no one knows better than the author, who took up the study of astrology in a spirit of the utmost hostility because challenged to know what he was talking about before he attacked it, how hard prejudice dies.

Anything, therefore, that can be done to overcome this indoctrination by demonstrating that the learned and the thoughtful have studied, believed and practiced astrology, is of value in establishing the right attitude of mind, without which all this must otherwise be merely an academic curiosity.

An understanding examination of the example charts which follow, in the light of the information which has preceded, should convince the reader that Vocational Astrology has an immense field of usefulness before it, the surface of which has been barely scratched.

Horoscope of *Business Man*

Birth Date *3/31/90* Time *5.11 a.m.*

True Local Time *5.03 a.m.*

Noon Mark *11:52 am*

Time to be adjusted / to the Noon Mark *6 hrs 49 mins earlier*

Time adj. *3 mos 19 das later*

Place _____

Lat. *52° 28' N* Long. *2° W*

	H.	M.	S.
Sideral Time previous noon	0	31	18
Add or subtract for difference in Longitude			1
Time Elapsed	17	3	
Add 10 secs. per hr. for time elapsed		2	51
	17	37	10

M. C. at Birth *17-37-10*

Adjusted Calculation Date *7/12/90*

Cardinal *☉ ♀ ♂ ♅* 6 8 / 7 0

Fixed *♃ ♄* 6 1P / 6 1

Common *☒ ☊ ℙ ☌ ☊* 5 0

Fiery *☉ ☽ ☒ ♀ ☌ ☊* 4 1

Earthy *1 ☊* 3 1P

Airy *♃ ♆ ♅ ℙ 1 ☊* 5 1P / 1

Watery *1 ☊* 3 1

Exalted *☉* 2 1

Essent. Dig. *None* 4 4P / 2

Accident Dig. *☉ ☒ ♀ ♅* 4 2

Critical Degree *None* = =

Fall *None* 3 1

Detriment *♀ ♄* = =

Ruler *♆ ♃ ♂* 0 1

Hyleg *☉*

46 4P / 12

10 FAV. 14 UNFAV.

ASPECTS

	☉	☽	☿	♀	♂	♃	♄	♅	♆	♇	Asc	MC	☊	☋	⊕
☉		☍	☌	♉	☌	⚹			☍	⚹		⚹	⚹		
☽	☍		10	10	1P	☍			☍	⚹		⚹	⚹		
☿	☌	10		☍					⚹	⚹		⚹	⚹		
♀	1P	10	☍				3 ⚹	⚹						△	
♂	☍	1P				△			⚹			⚹			
♃	⚹	⚹	⚹		△			⚹	4P	△					
♄				△				⚹	☍	△		△			
♅				⚹		⚹	⚹			ℙ		⚹	☌ ⚹		
♆	⚹	⚹	⚹		4P	☍				⚹					
♇	⚹	⚹	⚹		⚹	△	ℙ	☌							
Asc															
MC		☌		△		△	⚹							⚹	
☊															
☋													⚹		
⊕															

CHAPTER XVI

Horoscopes of the Successful
(*Continued*)

I.—A SUCCESSFUL BUSINESS MAN

THIS is the horoscope of a man engaged in a highly specialized wholesale business in which he is generally regarded as having been very successful. He is known nationally in his own particular trade circles as very expert in his line, or.e so difficult and hedged about with technical hazards that no direct competition exists and he has a virtual monopoly of the field.

Starting 30 years ago as Sales Correspondent in a somewhat similar business he worked his way through nearly all departments including road selling. His big "break" came when, after 7 years' experience, a wealthy individual in another city, desiring to start a similar business, offered him the position of General Sales Manager. Success was instantaneous and the new business flourished until hit by the post-war depression of 1921. In this year the native withdrew and organized his own Company, obtaining ample financial backing with small difficulty. The Company prospered until the Hoover depression of 1932–33 when bank closings and general conditions forced it to the wall. It was rescued by outside capital which had faith in the native and placed him in position to continue, though only at the expense of losing financial control and a cutting of one-half of his income. In the past seven years, after many setbacks, the native has again built up a solid structure and, though far from the size attained in the prosperous 'twenties, his business has made considerable headway and his income substantially increased. New difficulties, however, are crowding about him due to defense priorities and other troubles created by the war. He expresses confidence in his ability to overcome them as he has overcome those of the past.

There are some unusual features here, fully reflected in the horoscope. The native has followed one steady line for 30 years. We would expect to find ♄ concerned, as this planet rules not only business itself (the occupation) but is concerned with anything very much prolonged. Sure enough ♄ is in the sixth house (employment) and in close △ (very good) to the MidHeaven (occupation). The MidHeaven itself has 3 good aspects —one of them (from ♅) exact. ♅ is co-ruler with ☽ of the particular type of business in which the native is engaged.

But the MidHeaven has one fly in its otherwise clean ointment. That bugbear of all horoscopes, ☋, is in ♂. Now ☋ is a sort of lesser ♄ so far as malignancy is concerned. It does not govern anything, as ♄ does, but sends out a similar type malefic radiation on a smaller scale. It stops short of wreaking the actual ruin which ♄ delights in when in bad aspect or without aspect, but it can do pretty considerable damage for all that.

It is ☋ that is responsible for the native's repeated setbacks. Only the major ones have been cited but there are many minor ones attributable to this ☋ influence. Yet the native has weathered them thus far, due to the remarkable phenomenon of 50 good aspects and positions against only 14 bad ones. Some of these are quite exceptional as ☉ with 7 favorable aspects, exalted, and with not a single affliction, also strong in the angular first house. ☽ is almost as good, with 7 favorable against 1 unfavorable. And to add the final touch of good fortune, ☉ is exact △☽.

There is one curious lack, however, for a good business horoscope—the almost total dearth of earthy (practical) signs. This group is represented by only one minor angle. This has worked out in a rather significant fashion, and must be considered in connection with the overwhelming fiery signs which contain 6 planets and an angle—100% over average. Fiery signs confer intuition, long range vision and an almost uncanny ability, when very prominent, to pierce below the surface and play a "hunch" successfully.

The native is in a business so "impractical" that no one else will have anything to do with it. Yet he has sustained himself by it for 30 years—20 of them heading his own concern. His fiery signs showed him possibilities and methods of operation, no "level headed" business man with a horoscope full of earthy signs could see. His "hunches" rarely fail and he possesses a strange sort of prophetic faculty as to outcomes which his associates rely on without understanding. He is also a firm believer in astrology, which has helped him immeasurably.

The amazingly aspected ☉ has brought him much help from those in better position than himself, and in many cases unsought. ☉ rules influence and the influential, and his career has been greatly furthered in such ways. A badly afflicted ☉ rules out aid of this kind—the native has to do everything for himself and if his Ascendant is well aspected makes a very good job of it.

The unusual nature of his occupation—one with which the public at large is but little acquainted and about which many misunderstandings exist even in trade circles has several indicators. ♆ and ♅ together rule the unusual; ♇ governs the exclusive—that of which only one exists. Thus ♇ rules death, and a man can die but once. Under ♇'s government are dictators, and one dictator to a country (and now one to many countries) makes dictatorship a very exclusive profession. In individual horoscopes ♇, like ♅ and ♆, may have no good effects even when well aspected if the native is of the "backward" type. Everyone, however, responds to his bad aspects. These three planets seem to call for a certain above-average level of intellect or spirituality before their good side can manifest. Consequently it has to be determined, not from the horoscope alone but from some knowledge of the native and his background, whether or not the good aspects of this trio of "advanced" planets should be considered or ignored.

They may safely be taken where the native is an intelligent (not merely credulous) believer in astrology—where he has faith in the reality of a directive power in Nature—or even where he is only willing to concede that there is something "behind the scenes" and that the visible workings of the Universe do not constitute its sole reality. Many planets in fiery signs supply this realization as a matter of course. A large number in the watery group will do it in lesser degree. Earthy signs when preponderant mitigate against it. Airy signs may lead to such a conclusion from sheer hard thinking the matter through, but except for ♒, which has occult leanings, do not contribute to deep beliefs. Some knowledge of the native's background and an estimate of his degree of evolutionary advancement, apart from what the horoscope shows, is therefore desirable in attempting to evaluate the planets ♇, ♆ and ♅ from the standpoint of their good indications. In practice astrologers usually take them at face value where the client's own horoscope is under examination. Obviously he has some faith in the reality of the unseen or he would not be consulting them. But even here the degree of intelligence is to be considered. Blind, unreasoning faith is not necessarily the hallmark of advancement in evolution.

In the horoscope now being analyzed it is evident that these planets may be taken into full account. ♆ ☌ ♇ in the second house (money) clearly shows the unusual and exclusive nature of the money-making abilities. Both planets are within orb (5°) of the third house (mind) and exercise powerful influence upon it. They give the same out-of-the-ordinary slant to the mental processes. ♅ in exact ✳ the MidHeaven gives the final touch to this *flair* for the unusual in business and money-making activities. It is a fact that throughout the native's entire career he has never been successful in any line or occupation of a routine or well-understood nature. In merchandising, he has to devise methods which have never occurred to others. Even his business correspondence dispenses with the customary formalities and is attention-compelling by its staccato statements of fact and its keen appraisement of essentials. Irrelevancies are brushed aside, original points of

view developed, and in every department he contacts,
the native's efforts are surrounded with an aura of
♇-♆-♅. As a result the native is running what might
be termed a "one-man show," which it would be difficult, if not impossible, to carry on without him.

In this case ♄, though △ MidHeaven is entirely subordinate as a business indicator to ♅, though the latter
is only ✶. ♅ makes an exact aspect where ♄'s is nearly
3° out. ♅ is strong by house, being angular (seventh)
where ♄ is in a weak cadent house (sixth). ♅, while not
exalted or dignified by sign is at least not in any disability, while ♄ is in its detriment in ♌. ♄ is ✶♅
which is very good for both, yet ♅ has taken the lead
in coloring the native's business life with ♄ only as
runner-up. ♄, however, has played no inconsequential
part in aiding the native, even though inferior in importance to ♅. Its influence is plainly seen in the tenacity with which the native has followed one line of
business for 30 years. Only once during the entire period
(and then for only 30 days) did he take a flyer at something else—accepting a position as Credit Manager for
a large cereal house (♄, ruler of grains and cereals.)
The native spent the most unhappy month of his life
during this period, which followed his decision to leave
the road because of the lack of home life. Within 30
days, with Uranian suddenness and unexpectedness the
great opportunity heretofore described had opened up,
without any kind of effort on his part, and he was back
again in the Uranian field wherein he so obviously
belonged.

Here is a case where the ♅ ✶ MidHeaven (exact)
took precedence over all other business indicators in the

horoscope. Had the native consciously selected his field instead of being pushed into it by circumstances, themselves the product of the strong indicators, he might have made a choice even better than the course charted by ♅.

♐ is on the MidHeaven, with ♃, ruler, in ♒ on the cusp of the twelfth house but still retaining influence on the eleventh (hopes, wishes and ambitions) as it is not yet out of orb of the eleventh and its presence in ♒, eleventh house sign, adds greatly to this influence. The native has always felt a strong attraction to the occupations governed by ♃ and ♐, especially advertising, writing for publication and the publishing business. The presence of his co-ruler ♂ in ♐ and the powerfully aspected ♃ (6 good, 1 bad) has reinforced this attraction. The ☉ in ♐ and in the tenth house has, however, heretofore prevented this from being more than a sideline in his life. Advertising material is a tremendous factor in his business and he has always written such copy himself, relying on no outside agencies, and only in minor measure on assistants. He has written for magazines and newspapers and has had little difficulty in getting his material accepted. The perfect ☿ (5 good aspects, no bad, and strong in an angle—also nearest planet to Ascendant) shows writing ability. He also has been a prolific writer of sales manuals and bulletins and trade copy of various kinds. He edits and publishes in the interests of a semi-religious organization of which he is an officer, a small monthly magazine.

The interesting question is, if the native had selected his vocation consciously, as a result of an analysis of the horoscope, could he have made a greater success and (more important) would he have lived a happier life? The answer is, probably yes. Though in this case the horoscopic influences were so strong that they virtually pushed him into his career, the general rule is that greater success always follows deliberate choice based on knowledge rather than in blindly following what appear to be the lines of least resistance.

Furthermore, this type of horoscope is rather rare. Often the occupational indicators are so confused and conflicting that the native drifts from one thing to another, never quite finding himself, and ends up in some secondary occupation, which the horoscope may indeed show as a possibility but on which the influences sneer rather than smile.

The native could in all probability have developed into quite a successful writer, had he also taken into account his powerful ♇-♆-♅ cast of mind and have written along entirely original and unusual lines. He might have made a success in the advertising business, by the same methods—the out-of-ordinary. As he is still a comparatively young man, retaining plenty of energy, there is a not remote possibility that he may yet exploit that particular side of his occupational possibilities, which thus far he has barely scratched.

The malevolent interference of ☋ in ♐ and in the tenth must not be overlooked. Probably the sidetracking of Sagittarian occupations and concentration on things indicated by the ♅-MidHeaven ✳ were astrologically brought about by this horoscopic killjoy. Yet one compensating advantage of ☋ in tenth house is that in consequence ☊ must be in the fourth house which governs outcomes, and also the latter years of the life.

The frequent setbacks ☊ has caused have been mentioned earlier, but ☋ in a curious and at times almost uncanny fashion has guided the outcome even of the most unpromising situation to a satisfactory conclusion.

The native could have been born with a horoscope which might have taken him much farther, but he might have fared much worse. He is happy in his work, with a keen zest for life and an understanding of what it means, which goes far to compensate him for the minor annoyances and irritations of his bad aspects. And so he is cited as an example of a successful business man—not wealthy—not outstanding (except in his own circle)—not yet with his future fully assured. But satisfied with his chosen work, still ambitious and with plenty of *joie de vivre* left, and if success consists in having these things, therefore successful.

TWENTY YEARS AFTER

The native retired from his wholesale commodity business several years ago after being in it for 38 years and in the same line for others ten additional years (♄ △ M C). He has turned to good account the unafflicted ☿ (five favorable, no unfavorable aspects) and formed his own publishing company (♃ , six good aspects, 1 adverse; ♂ in ♐ , four good, one bad, ♂ being a life ruler).

He has written and successfully marketed several "best sellers," all along unconventional and original lines (♆ and ♇ on cusp of third house; ♆ , five good, three bad; ♇ , four good, three bad). Both ♆ and ♇ are ⚹ ♃ . The "small monthly magazine" he edits and publishes which likewise deals with ♅ - ♆ affairs is still small in size but very much greater in circulation and influence

than when the original reference to it was made. It now
has an international circulation and is quoted in periodi-
cals as far off as India and New Zealand.

The ♅ - ♃ ✳ has also given his activities, and more
especially those of the organization with which he is connected, a very great amount of favorable publicity via TV
and radio. He has had both his own program and scores
of interviews by invitation. Now in his seventies he is as
active as at any period of his life and with the benefic ♌
in the fourth house (declining years) and the excellent ☿
governing ♊ on the fourth house cusp, this productive
activity may reasonably be expected to continue well into
old age.

CHAPTER XVII

Horoscopes of the Successful
(*Continued*)

2.—A SUCCESSFUL CLUBWOMAN

THE Clubwoman is a peculiarly American phenomenon, the product—and a healthy one—of the more ample leisure which the labor-saving devices of this generation permit to its womenfolk. It is an outgrowth of the gregarious instinct among women which, in less sophisticated times, expressed itself in the sewing circle, the prayer meeting and the "coffee-klatsch." But it also expresses, and in much greater measure, the desire to be of service to the world.

"Clubwomanism," if such a term is permissible, is now one of the country's major "industries," rating respectful notice from pulpit and press. Its keynote was ably summed up in an address given by a well known clergyman at the Triennial Convention of the General Federation of Women's Clubs, attended by 6000 women representing a membership of two million throughout the country. He termed it "the very genius of women at work for themselves and with themselves to strengthen America and to help build a better world."

The horoscope selected is that of a woman peculiarly fitted for this type of endeavor, possessing the requisite leisure to follow such avocation. She is happy in this

work and because of the special nature of the horoscope
has advanced in it without any ambitious effort of her
own. She has volunteered her service freely and gladly
to those particular branches which interested her, but
has made no attempt whatever to advance herself in
office in any of the several clubs with which she has been
associated. Yet preferment has come to her unsought
and even undesired. Her interest is in the work itself
and in no way in the limelight of office.

At present she occupies the presidency of a large and
active literary society, is past president of another leading club and district chairman of the Art Section of the
Federation. She is a member of several other clubs and
a landscape artist of merit. In the past she has held
numerous offices and directorships in other women's
clubs, some of them political. She is well liked and en-
joys a wide circle of friendships.

The horoscope shows the very earnest and sincere
♐ rising—a sign possessing great altruism and desire to
be of use. ☉ is in the capable ♑ and ☽ in ♈, which
delights in leadership. The heavily afflicted ☉ (4 bad
aspects, 1 good) has been of little help to the native in
providing influence from those in higher station to push
her forward—such as was so prominent in the business
man's horoscope. The native has risen entirely by her
own efforts and by favor found with her equals, especially with friends. ☽'s 5 good aspects against 3 bad
ones are significant in this respect, the good including
a △ to ♀, well within orb of the eleventh house
(friends) and on the cusp of the twelfth (clubs and
societies). ☽ is also in exact △ to ☿ in the twelfth and

close ♂ ♃, the ruler. It also has a ✳ to ♆, club planet
and to ♇.

The Literary Club presidency is clearly marked in
the ☽– ☿ △, which also denotes a good mentality.
☿ is highly favored by both benefics, being parallel ♀
and exact △ ♃. The practical side of the mind is enhanced and considerable power of concentration shown
by the close ☿ ✳ ♄. The airy element (mentality) is
well represented by 3 planets and 2 angles. The native
would have reached great intellectual heights were it
not for the poor placement by both sign and house of
☿ (detriment and cadent twelfth house). This sets
bounds to the mental achievements, while the two ☍'s
of ☿ to ♆ and ♇, the former reinforced by parallel,
give a certain measure of frustration to the efforts.
♇ and ♆ both in the sixth (health) house, the native
has been greatly handicapped in the past by ailments
which have slowed up her efforts, though this disability
appears now to have been overcome.

Any planet in the MidHeaven tends to cause the
native to rise above the station in which he was born,
as does also ☉ in the first house, both of which conditions exist here. ☉ does not help much because of its
afflictions but ♄ with 5 good aspects against 3 bad and
in its exaltation (stronger for good than for evil) has
materially aided the native in her climb from small
beginnings. An afflicted ♄ as all astrologers know, will,
when on the MidHeaven, raise a native to high station
but at long last bring him crashing down to ruin. It is
this position of ♄ in Hitler's horoscope which astrologers claim is the ultimate hope of civilization to be

rid of him and his system. [♄ in tenth □ ♀ (4) □ ♂ (4) P ♂, against only one light ✳ ♅ (7)]

In our clubwoman's chart, however, no such catastrophe is to be feared, as the good far outweighs the bad in this key occupational planet.

Many years ago when clubwork was probably the farthest thing from her mind, an astrologer stated that there was considerable evidence in the natal chart that prominence would be achieved in political and social work. At that time the native's interests lay in wholly other directions and it hardly seemed possible either to her or her family that such a changed state of affairs could come about.

But horoscopic indicators, when powerful enough, have a way of coming into their own, and in due season the astrologer's opinion was justified by events. Greater successes in this field lie before the native if she takes full advantage of the wider possibilities the horoscope permits. But man has freewill and it is strictly up to her.

TWENTY YEARS AFTER

The possibilities indicated in the closing paragraph of the foregoing delineation have come to pass in full measure. The planet ♄ exalted in ♎ ✳ ♀ has extended the art interests into a far wider field. Now recognized as one of the outstanding women artists of the area she was awarded last year by a jury of art experts from out-of-town, a citation and subsequently first prize of $200.00 for the best pastel of the season.

The four good aspects of ♀ coupled with the twelfth house position of both ♀ and ☿ (institutions) have been astrologically responsible for her taking a major part in organizing a Women Artists Society (of which she became first President) with a distinguished and respected membership.

This is a good example of a horoscope, the potentialities of which have been in large measure fulfilled in spite of a considerable number of adverse aspects which at times have placed formidable obstacles in the way.

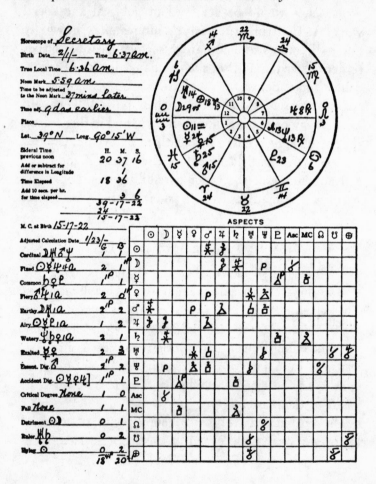

CHAPTER XVIII

Horoscopes of the Successful
(*Concluded*)

3.—A SUCCESSFUL SECRETARY

THE native has been connected with one concern virtually her entire business life, (17 years). She was hired as an extra typist for temporary work only but, showing efficiency and intelligence far above the average, she was retained as stenographer, later being promoted to secretarial work to which much later were added the duties of office manager. Eventually she became Secretary to the President of the Company and recently, while continuing to retain this position, was also elected Secretary-Treasurer and a Director of the concern.

Ample leadership is shown by 4 planets, including the ruler, ♅ and ☽ in cardinal signs. There is great tenacity of purpose and considerable willpower, as evidenced by ☉, ☿ (mind planet), ♃ and all 4 angles fixed. The natural Aquarian friendliness is reinforced by 3 planets common, including the subordinate ruler, ♄. The native is a double Aquarian, having both Ascendant and ☉ there. ☽ in ♑ gives shrewd business sense. ☿ exalted in ♒, coupled with adequate airy signs, supplies quick, alert intelligence. ☽ ♂ Ascendant is also indicator of a responsive mind.

The native's long service with one Company is shown out by the same indicator as in the case of the Business Man's horoscope (Chapter XVI) by ♄ △ MidHeaven. She has excellent taste and a real *flair* for artistry in clothes. ♀ is exalted in ♓ with an almost exact ☒ ♅ and △ ♆. These two planets confer an original idea of design and ornament so pronounced that her milliner recently offered her a partnership if she would come into the business with him, an offer promptly refused for reasons which will be made manifest further on.

An indefatigable worker, the native supplements her income by work as spare time Secretary to a journalist and by specialized routine editorial work. ♃ △ ♂ in second house, though light, shows this particular source of income. ♃ rules journalism and ♂ in second gives good earning power. ♂ seldom holds on to his accumulations however. The native also has ♄ in the second. This planet is the exact antithesis of ♂ and is quite thrifty. The native is a curious mixture of thrift and extravagance, following out the indications of both these second house planets. Her employers have sufficient confidence in the former quality to leave a good deal of routine buying in her hands, and have never found occasion to criticize her for paying too much. Yet should some particular article of feminine adornment especially appeal to her she is likely to cast financial discretion to the winds and spend the painful savings of several months in an afternoon. The Saturnine thrift shows out in the fact that even here she will invariably obtain the best possible value for her money.

The "clothes complex" is indicated by the excellently placed ♀ exactly on the cusp of the second (money)

house. ♀, lesser benefic, so placed also gives good earning capacity. The native is little likely to come to want
as the fourth house (latter years) has ♉, money sign,
ruled by ♀, on the cusp.

In handling office help the native is considerate yet
very firm, the cardinal-fixed signs showing out to best
advantage. Both of the Company officials for whom
she worked as Secretary had ☉ in ♈, and it will be
noted that ♂, ruler of ♈, is in ♈ in second house and
✳ her own ☉. ♂ is also parallel ♀ (money) and light
△ the great benefic ♃ in ♌. Ruler of her present employer's Ascendant is ♃ and his ☽ is in ♌.

The right vocation (Secretary) is clearly indicated
by the ♏ MidHeaven. ♇, ruler of ♏, is virtually exact
△ and also parallel ☿ which rules secretarial work. It
is true ♇ also has a □ to ♄ (the business) and it is a
fact that certain features of her work, having to do
with collections, lawsuits and the like are distasteful to
the native. This does not prevent her from handling
them with first-rate efficiency.

Both of the executives for whom the native worked
have taken considerable interest in helping her improve
her general cultural background. Starting with only an
eighth-grade education plus considerable native intelligence, she lost no opportunity of adding to her knowledge of English and acquiring those niceties of expression and comprehension which are the mark of the
educated. Today few college graduates express themselves more aptly or with greater ease of manner. This,
coupled with a cultured speaking voice and an excellent
all-around knowledge, has been a source of the most
intense satisfaction to the native who regards the con-

tacts which made it possible as the most important asset of her position.

In declining the offer of the partnership in the Millinery firm, she stressed this as the principal reason for her refusal.

The native is unmarried, several romances having been broken up by her parents because of difference in faith. ☉, co-ruler of marriage, is in close ☍ to ♃ which rules religion. ♂, the other marriage ruler, is in very close □ both to ♅, which shatters when in bad aspect and ♆ which frustrates. ♆ is also ruler of the Church of which the native is a communicant and which frowns on mixed marriages. ♆, however, is also in nearly exact △ ♀ and absolutely exact ☌ ☊. The native is devout in her religion both in belief and practice. The religious house (ninth) has ♎ on cusp and is therefore governed by ♀ which, however is close ⚹ ♅, though △ ♆. While adhering to all the rites and customs of her belief (♆) the native has a considerable *flair* for the occult (♅) and feels that it enables her to understand her own faith better because of the light it casts on otherwise obscure teachings.

With all the order and method of her many fixed signs, the native retains the fun-loving Aquarian disposition, and at times is somewhat incomprehensible to her more staid acquaintances and even to her own family. The two odd planets ♅ and ♆, almost exactly ☍ each other, add this curious quirk to the character which at base, however, is well grounded and down to earth. The native is far from being the stodgy secretary of novels and movies. She is athletic (♂ strong) and has captained a soft ball and basket ball team, plays an excellent contract bridge game and lives a thoroughly rounded out life.

She is likely to rise much higher, both in business and social life.

TWENTY YEARS AFTER

The native is still associated with the same enterprise, completely reorganized and in a different type of production. Her thinking and general outlook has continued to mature, the excellent Mercury, exalted, parallel and almost exact trine Pluto having fulfilled its promise. The reasoning powers and the capacity for well-considered judgments have broadened and deepened with the years, so that her opinions and counsel are always given weight whenever expressed.

This good all-around horoscope has bright assurance for the latter years, as Taurus is on the cusp of the fourth house that rules the culminating period of the life. There is no planet in the house but the exalted Venus in Pisces rules Taurus and therefore stands for the house ruler. It has two very close good aspects, one of which is a trine to the ruler Uranus. Aside from a parallel to Mars, not of much consequence, there are no afflictions to Venus. A fortunate augury for comfort and security in the years to come.

CHAPTER XIX

Horoscopes of World Figures

1.—A PRESIDENT OF THE UNITED STATES

2.—A DICTATOR

3.—A PRIME MINISTER OF GREAT BRITAIN

IN THIS and the two following chapters abridged horoscopes and short vocational delineations are given of the following outstanding characters, each a typical representative of his chosen line of endeavor:

1. A President of the United States
2. A Dictator
3. A Prime Minister of Great Britain
4. An Oil Millionaire
5. A Financier
6. A Pioneer in Medical Research
7. A Playwright
8. An Artist
9. An Inventor
10. A USSR Dictator
11. A Vice-President of the United States
12. A Governor of New York

Attention is drawn only to the most significant features of the chart. It is recommended that the student set up the horoscope in each case in detail, calculating all aspects, positions, etc., and then make his own full delineation based on the astrological laws set forth in earlier chapters.

I.—FRANKLIN D. ROOSEVELT

PRESIDENT OF THE UNITED STATES

♅ almost exactly on the Ascendant, coupled with ♂ and ☽ in tenth—6 of the 10 planets high up in the chart and another on the ascending angle—mark a character of great power, almost certain to rise in life. ♃ in virtually exact △ ♅ from his own house, the ninth, ♃ also being △ Ascendant, ♆ having similar △'s from ninth, precipitates foreign affairs most forcefully into the life.

The native gains much from these powerful aspects and positions—the third term was probably due to them—yet ♄ on cusp of ninth □ ☉ and ♀, and ☋ near the MidHeaven, constitute a major threat from this same source.

Mr. Roosevelt's strong ☿, exalted in ♒, rules both Ascendant and MidHeaven. His tenth house ♂ trines ☿ exact. There is no "Presidential Horoscope." Thousands of other natives born with closely similar horoscopes did not become Presidents of the United States. They might, and many of them probably did, become Presidents of Companies, organizations, societies, or other institutions. ♂ and ☽ both in tenth, ♂ being exact △ to ruler, gives enormous drive which, if the balance of the horoscope is reasonably favorable, can hardly fail to lift the native high in his field, whatever it may be.

Note ☽ is also very strong—essentially dignified in ♋. ♀ is ♂ ⊕. The president is a wealthy man. ☉ also conjoins ⊕. All are in fifth (investments). ♀ rules

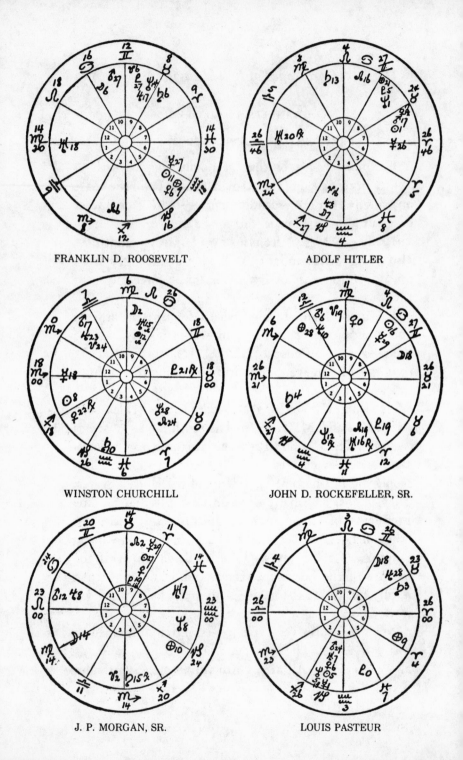

FRANKLIN D. ROOSEVELT

ADOLF HITLER

WINSTON CHURCHILL

JOHN D. ROCKEFELLER, SR.

J. P. MORGAN, SR.

LOUIS PASTEUR

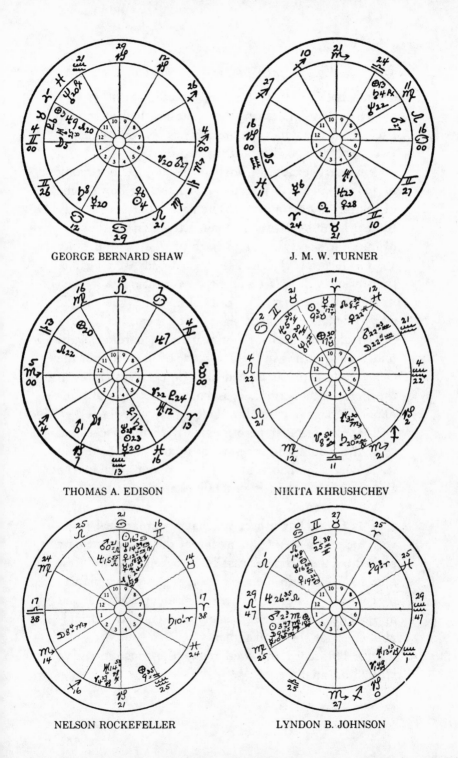

GEORGE BERNARD SHAW

J. M. W. TURNER

THOMAS A. EDISON

NIKITA KHRUSHCHEV

NELSON ROCKEFELLER

LYNDON B. JOHNSON

second, both normally (♉) and because ♎, other sign of ♀, is on second cusp. Yet there are bad afflictions from ♄ in its fall. The native has, however, nearly twice as many good aspects as bad ones.

☽ is nearly exact △ MidHeaven—another testimony of advancement. ☽ is exact ✳ ♄, cutting down some of the latter's malignancy. The native battled his way to health (♂ △ ☿ exact) against the terrible affliction of infantile paralysis (☿ in sixth parallel ♆ and exact □ ♇ in detriment). The astrological odds were against him in spite of ☿'s excellent sign position.

The balance was doubtless turned by the terrific array of planets in fixed signs—7 of them.

The almost total lack of planets in cardinal signs may seem puzzling in the horoscope of the leader of the country. It explains a good deal that is mysterious in the President's actions. It is known that he waits for public opinion to crystallize before taking action—then he shapes his course accordingly. With many cardinal signs, he would be far ahead of it and seek to mould it. Advisers probably play a far greater part in the President's life than is generally known.

A man can rise without cardinal signs, if other aspects favor, but others will have a great deal to do with his policies. An explanation of the prominent part played by the "Brain Trust" and other trusted "New Dealers" is seen in the 4 comon angles plus 2 planets in common. They make the President likeable and approachable without noticeably weakening the formidable effect of the fixed signs.

This horoscope will well repay the most intensive study and analysis.

2.—ADOLF HITLER

DICTATOR OF NAZI GERMANY

In the horoscope of a nation's ruler, particularly of one whose word is so absolute as that of the German fuehrer, the houses, signs and planets assume a national significance and are to be interpreted not merely with reference to the private affairs of the individual but of the nation whose destiny is bound up with his.

It is interesting, therefore, to note that the terrific opposition felt for Hitler's ideas all over the civilized world is expressed in his natal chart in as full a measure as the greatest stickler for astrological consistency could ask. The seventh house (public enemies) and the sign ♎ (normal to seventh house) are the ones we would expect to find involved, and they are the most prominent factors in the chart. The former contains 4 of the 10 planets (40% of the whole as against an average of 8⅓%). The latter is the ascending sign and also contains the powerful ♅. This appears in the twelfth house (secret enemies). In the house of death (the eighth) which has played so great a part in the fuehrer's bloody career, are ♇, planet of death and ♆, which so often makes its appearance in lethal matters. ⊕, which marks the source from which the greatest material accumulations come, is, significantly enough, in the sign ♊ (writings) and in the house of mortality. Hitler's entire income is said to be derived from the sale of millions of copies of his book, *Mein Kampf*, which preaches woe, destruction and death to all who oppose him. Significant, too, is ☊ in the ninth (publications).

It is said that Hitler's great ambition was to be an artist and that he still cherishes the hope that his later years may be devoted to this peaceful occupation. Those in position to judge state that he has some talent along artistic lines, though far from a genius. ♀ (art) is strong in its own sign (♉), though retrograde, which would push this possibility into the future. There are other reasons why Hitler may never realize it, one being the □ of ♄ to ♀ (4° of orb), the other the exact ♂ ♂. ♎, the Ascendant, is the most artistic of signs and although it has been disparagingly said that Hitler was a housepainter and paperhanger "and not a very good one," the horoscope shows that he *was* probably a very good one.

The extraordinary placement of ♂ and ♀, planets of war and peace respectively, in the identical degree and sign and in the seventh house, both □ ♄ and with no other aspects, is an omen of hope for the world. While the benefic ♀ gives ♂ (war) every aid and comfort, at long last ♄ will smash down the whole evil structure.

In starting his various drives, Hitler, who is said to be a most competent astrologer or very well advised, seems to set great store by good aspects to his ☽-♃ position in 7°–8° ♑. These planets are unafflicted and, while neither is well placed by sign, he evidently regards them as the best offset he has to his malignant ♄, as they are in the Saturnine sign ♑. That his judgment has been amazingly good is shown by the uncanny success of his belligerent enterprises. German thoroughness and planning, of course, technical efficiency, years of preparation, ruthless execution letting nothing stand in the way—all these were present and the other side had little to oppose them with except steadfastness and courage. But they were present in the last World War in as great measure relatively speaking, and the other side had still less at the outset. What is the missing factor which has made the German war-machine thus far so nearly invincible? We say it is the fuehrer's knowlege of astrology.

His enemies concede him a superb sense of timing. From whence does this come? No human being, not even a Hitler, can by ordinary standards be sure of not making one false guess when planning moves which bring in so many bewildering factors. We know of no way it can be done, other than by expert use of astrology. ♄ will wear Hitler down at last, but it may be a very long last if he continues to stay out of ♄'s realm by staking everything on Uranian blitzkriegs and surprises. No planet can function if not given material to work with. ♄ needs lengthy periods of time and, preferably, orthodox, routine-like methods, long established and well understood. Time fights against him, it is true, but he is doing a remarkable job of ducking and keeping out of its way. That, with all his cunning, he has miscalculated the ultimate eventuality is shown by ☿ ☍ Ascendant, exact.

To later readers of this book the outcome of the war and Hitler's fate may no longer be the mystery it is as these words are penned. But whatever that outcome and that fate may be, in the convinced opinion of the author, ♄ will be (astrologically) the greatest contributory factor.

3.—WINSTON CHURCHILL

PRIME MINISTER OF GREAT BRITAIN

In perfect contrast to Hitler, Mr. Churchill's ☿ is exactly on the Ascendant. This brilliant meteor of British politics has been soldier, writer, statesman and is now leader of the British people in their most hazardous period since England became a nation. His Ascendant is ♏, most unyielding of all the signs. His mind (☿) is also cast in the ♏ mould, and ♇, ruler of ♏, is in ♉ and opposing the Ascendant (3° orb). 4 planets and 2 angles fixed exactly equal Hitler's 4 planets, 2 angles in the same constitution. He cannot boast of the same showy leadership as Hitler who has 4 planets, 2 angles in cardinal signs against Churchill's scant 3 planets and no angles. Hitler calls for loyalty to Hitler as leader—Churchill to Britain as country. We have seen no word of demand from him for loyalty to himself, though this is magnificently bestowed without being asked, by his embattled people.

One does not deliberately train to become a Prime Minister, President of the United States or Fuehrer. These are positions to which men are called (or, in the case of the last named, force themselves). Looking at a natal chart, no matter how good, one cannot say at the child's birth, "This is the horoscope of a President or Prime Minister." Others born at approximately the same time and place will have similar horoscopes. A superbly muscled young man with a powerful constitution may or may not choose to exploit his physical perfection by becoming a prizefighter or athlete. He has the equipment. What he chooses to do with it may depend upon his own choice or upon external circumstances over which he may have little control. Similarly the horoscope shows possibilities; and the greatness or littleness of the soul behind, will determine to what extent they are used. Winston Churchill, born to the purple, son of a leader of the House of Commons, educated at Harrow and Sandhurst, could hardly have failed to make some kind of a mark unless he had an extremely bad horoscope. As a matter of fact he has a very good one and has exploited its possibilities well-nigh to the utmost.

His success as a soldier is shown by ♂ (war) ☌ ♃ and ✳ ♀. As a writer his ♃ ✳ ♀ from ♎ (sign of ♀) to ♐ (sign of ♃) points to outstanding recognition. These planets, being in each other's signs are in what is called "mutual receptivity," greatly adding to their power. As a statesman ☽ ✳ ♄ (2° orb) and ☉ in the strong first house, amply accounts for his long stay in politics. Yet ☉ □ ☽, though rather light (6°), has threatened his prestige many times and is likely to threaten it again.

The harrowing threat from abroad is plainly shown out by ♅ in ninth house (foreign affairs) ☍ ♄ (5°). It is not strong, but strong enough to cause plenty of trouble. England's worries on the seas are aptly typified by ♆ (sea) ☍ ♃ foreign affairs planetary ruler, and in ♎ (strife). ♃ itself is almost on top of the snarling ☋. Yet ♆ conjoins ♌—a good luck token for the British Navy.

With ♀ in second house (money) Churchill could hardly be anything but well off, and all the aspects of

♀ contribute to this happy state of affairs. Churchill is said by his intimates to be "enjoying the war hugely." With ♂ ☌ ♃ in the eleventh house (hopes, wishes and ambitions) this is understandable. ♐ in which he has his ☉, is humane, as is ♍ where ☽ is posited. There is, however, nothing especially humane about ♏, nor about ♉ where his ruler ♇ appears. His co-ruler ♂ is in ♎, a gentle sign when left alone but vicious when blended with ♂.

This most historic character will certainly leave a profound impress on both British and international history, but wars have proved graveyards of many great reputations, and Mr. Churchill will need every resource his fine heritage and splendid background provide him to escape all of the lurking pitfalls his natal chart indicates as probably lying before him.

CHAPTER XX

Horoscopes of World Figures
(*Continued*)

4.—AN OIL MILLIONAIRE

5.—A FINANCIER

6.—A PIONEER IN MEDICAL RESEARCH

4.—JOHN D. ROCKEFELLER, SR.
OIL MILLIONAIRE

Aᴳᴬᴵᴺ ♏ is rising, and the ruthlessness with which the native crushed competition in the days during which he was building up his oil empire required this hefty sign for its full expression. ♂, co-ruler of ♏, is in the tenth, occupational house, very close ✳ ♄ in first. This gives terrific drive in business matters. The planets are so arranged as to give the native aid in almost anything he does connected with his material affairs. ♂ is in the tenth ☌ ♃; ♃ is ✳ ♄. ♅, ruler of tenth, is △ Ascendant, also ✳ ♂. Very seldom do the planets and signs so conspire together to smooth a business path.

At that it was not all smooth. ☋ in tenth not far from MidHeaven subjected him to tremendous public criticism, though it in no way affected his steady progress to millionairedom.

It is interesting to trace the astrological correspondences which can be found every step of the way along this native's monumental career. At 16 he became an assistant bookkeeper, a ♍ occupation. On the cusp of the sixth (employment) is ♉, money sign, ruled by ♀ which is in ♏. This was for a commission house, a business ruled by ♄. ♀ is □ ♄ (4° orb), and weak in ♏. The native earned $50 for the first three months of his employment, after which he was advanced to $25 per month. Even for those days these were "starvation" wages.

As evidence that an insignificant start under the worst aspects may lead to great things, the native somehow managed to save enough in three years to buy a partnership in a produce firm. He was no longer an employee and his poor employee aspects (which by incredible self-sacrifice he used for good) disappear from the picture henceforth. He was never an employee again. The first foundations of his career were, however, from employment and from money earned in employment. In this regard, ♍, employment sign, on the MidHeaven, and ♉, money sign, on the employment house are most significant.

He became a partner, and the ☽ occupying the seventh (partnership) house took over. ♉ is on the cusp but a planet in any house except the first always takes precedence of the sign. In the first only when within 5° of the Ascendant, and not always then if the rising sign be fixed. The connection between the employment and the partnership, the one leading to the other is, however, clearly indicated by the same sign, ♉, being on the cusp of both the sixth and the seventh.

Rockefeller made a good investment in his partnership. In the fifth house (investments) is his ruler, ♇,

almost exact ✳ ☽ in seventh. ☽ also △'s ♃ in partnership sign, ♎, and in tenth (business) house—a perfect
setup. It is, too, △ ♆, and its one bad aspect, a ☐ ♅,
is insufficient to upset this congeries of good ones. Four
years later he and his partner were able to invest
$4,000 in an infant oil refining business. Here ♆, ruling
oil, △ ☽, also ruling oil, the former being in ♒, the sign
of new processes, clearly marked the path the native
traveled.

Why was ♅, then, so quiescent, with its close ☐ ☽?
Why did it not upset things or at least bring about
some kind of difficulty? Doubtless all was not such plain
sailing as a bald narration of the facts would indicate,
but astrologically the power of a malefic to harm is
largely nullified by a ♂ ☊. ♅ here conjoins ☊ within
3° and its efforts by ☐ to frustrate the △'s and ✳'s
are in consequence almost impotent. ☊ in fourth is a
consolation prize for having ☋ in tenth. It smiles on
"outcomes," no matter how unpromising the beginnings
may be, as evidence Rockefeller's pitiable starting wage
which developed into hundreds of millions.

Eight years more saw Rockefeller and his partners
(he had another one by then) doing 20 percent of all the
oil refining business in Cleveland, chief oil refining city
of the United States. He organized a million dollar
corporation (enormous for those times), holding more
than 25 percent of the stock himself. ♃ (ruling ♐ on
cusp of second) ✳ ♄ (ruling ♑ intercepted in second)
was beginning to tell. He was on his way.

It has been mentioned in a previous chapter that ♇
governs the exclusive. Its ✳ ☽ is of great moment in
this chart. It is virtually exact and ♇ is in the invest-

ment house. ☽ is Rockefeller's co-ruler due to ☉ in ♋.
♇ is the other ruler (♏ rising). ♇ rules monopoly and
Rockefeller was perhaps the first great monopolist in
America. By a series of shrewd moves Rockefeller induced the railroads to grant huge rebates to his Company and other refiners who were members of an association he formed, while at the same time they placed
penalties, or "drawbacks" as they were called, on all
oil shipped by non-members. By this method he forced
21 out of 26 competing refiners to sell out to Standard
Oil, his new Corporation.

☊ came charging forward with full malignancy, caus-
ing a storm of public indignation which forced the railroads to withdraw their agreement, but it was too late.
The object had already been achieved and Standard
Oil owned the Companies. Here it may be seen how a
malefic influence may work adversely but not suffi-
ciently so to upset stronger benefic influences. The
same would apply of course on the other side, were the
malefics in the superior position.

A few years more saw the native controlling 90 percent of the country's oil refineries.

It is not practicable to pursue his career at further
length here, but in spite of many legal difficulties due
to ♌ on cusp of ninth (law) ruled by ☉ □ ♇, ♀ ruler
of seventh (litigation) □ ♄ and the aforesaid ☊ in
tenth, no significant damage ever resulted to the native.
He was reputed at his retirement to be the richest man
in the country.

A word may be said regarding his enormous benefac-
tions, reaching upwards of half a billion dollars. Charity
is ruled by the twelfth house, ♃ and ♆. There is no

planet in the twelfth so ♇ and ♂ assume primary rulership as ♏ is on the cusp. ♂♂♃, ♇✳♆ and ☊ in ♓ (twelfth house sign) signify his great hearted generosity in this respect—surely of so much benefit to the human race that a grateful public may well consign to oblivion the memory of the hard dealings of the native's earlier life, when all was fair in business as in war.

5.—J. P. MORGAN, SR.

INTERNATIONAL FINANCIER

This native, born with the regal ☊ rising and his ruler, ☉, exalted in the leadership sign ♈ along with 3 other planets, was fortune's favorite from his first cry.

Exactly on cusp of second (money) house is ☽ within 1° of exact ✳ of ♄. On cusp of tenth is money sign, ♉. Highest in the chart stands benefic ☊. The native was born to money, received every educational and cultural advantage money could provide, and from his earliest manhood was an important figure in the banking and financial world. His ninth house (foreign matters) contains no fewer than 4 planets and ☊, and all his life his affairs constantly involved foreign countries. He was even educated at the University of Gottingen in Germany.

His financing of many railroads is shown by ♎ (ruler ♀) on cusp of third (transportation), ♀ being in ninth, a co-ruler in general of railroads, steamship lines and other institutions out of which the Morgan millions were garnered. Even the U. S. Government was beholden to him when, in 1895, he supported a tottering Treasury reserve by furnishing over $60,000,000 in gold. ☿ rules U. S. and is close ♂ native's ☉ (gold). ☉ is ♂ ♀.

♇, planet of monopoly, is also ♂ ♀, which is not good for ♀ but excellent for ♇. By itself ♀, which is not over-strong, could not have accounted for Morgan's wealth, but the unexcelled (for money) position of ☽ needed little reinforcement from the normal money planet.

Highest planet in the horoscope is ☿ ♂ ♌ ♂ ☉ (too close for eloquence, but the native was not famous for this), with no afflictions. The native's keen intellect overt wered all others in his field. He was a generous giver, his co-ruler, ♂, being in the twelfth house (charity) and ♃, planet of benevolence, being also there. ☽ rules sign on twelfth cusp (♋) and its paramount monetary influence has already been stressed.

Last, but supreme over all, is the main aspect which made J. P. Morgan the financial wizard of his generation and perhaps of all time. ☽, whose stellar role in his financial affairs dwarfs everything else in the horoscope, is exact △ his MidHeaven. Money was his business, and a fortunate business it was. True ♄ opposes Mid-Heaven but a planet ☍ its own sign or house has much of its malefic effect removed by the "throw-over" effect of opposite signs. Morgan built up his business the hard Saturnine way regardless of all the advantages of his environment and training. The country is indebted to him for the magnificent art collection left to the Metropolitan Museum of Art. That his judgment of art was not always of the best the ♀ in detriment ♂ ♇ position seems to show; but as a very rich man he could command the opinion of experts and could afford to be wrong sometimes.

He followed the natural lines of the horoscope, doing those things for which the horoscope best fitted him, hence his natal chart is ideal for vocational study.

6.—LOUIS PASTEUR

GREAT MEDICAL RESEARCH WORKER

Of all the horoscopes we have selected for vocational analysis this one is the most staggering to the imagination. No fewer than 6 planets are in the third house (mentality) and in the sign ♑. This is 60 percent of the whole. Allowing 10 planets for twelve houses, but taking into account that ☿ and ♀ stay close to ☉ and frequently are found in the same house, this is still far above the normal horoscope. The author does not recall, out of hundreds of students who have passed through his classes, a single one with 6 planets either in a single sign or house. Eight of the 10 planets also are in earthy signs.

To add to the potency of the third house, if any addition were needed, ☽ is in the third house sign, ♊. Here is a native who is obviously a mental genius, with a mind equipped to tackle almost any task requiring the most intense study and concentration. A lesser character than Pasteur might not be able to stand the terrific strain of so many planets in the mind house and might have cracked, becoming some kind of a psychopathic case. Pasteur, however, could not only "take it," he could use it. The well balanced ♎ Ascendant doubtless aided him. Even so, his tastes appear to have been a trifle peculiar. Thus at 16, when preparing for college in a school away from home, his health broke down and he begged to be sent home. His father was a tanner of hides, a peculiarly Saturnine occupation. Young Pasteur with so many planets in ♄'s sign, ♑, and itself △ nearly all of them, assured his instructors that if he could only smell the tannery once more he would soon be well. With most people the reverse would be the case.

Pasteur scrupulously, if unconsciously, followed his natural tendencies as indicated by the natal chart. His first money was earned as a teacher of mathematics (♄, ruler, in ♉, money sign). ♑'s insatiable appetite for work is well known. With almost his entire horoscope one gigantic ♑, Pasteur might be expected to exemplify this *in excelsis*. He did. "Throughout his entire life," reads a biographical sketch, "work was his constant inspiration." ♑ is tremendously ambitious. No sign places a higher premium on success. It is not, therefore, surprising to find him writing to his sisters, "These three things, will, work and success, between them fill human existence." That he had plenty of will is shown by 2 planets and 2 angles in fixed signs which together with the tyrannous ♑, which has all the tenacity in the world of its own, gave him his full share of the first quality on his list. His favorite words, said to be the last words he uttered, were, "*Il faut travailler*: It is necessary to work." The perfect ♑ native, in life or death.

The curious way in which the various researches which interested him and commanded his absorbed attention match up with the third house indicators may be briefly pointed out. One of his earliest researches was into the nature of a certain acid, involving examination of two types of crystals. Acids and crystals are ruled by ♄ and ♄'s sign ♑. Later he delved into the mysteries then surrounding diseases of beer and wine, both under the general rulership of ♆ in third house. Beer comes under ♄, being made with grain, and partly under ☽ (fermentation). ☽ is in third house sign, ♊. Wine is ruled by ♀ in third house. In 1864 Pasteur announced his atmospheric germ theory (germs ruled by ☽).

The uniqueness and originality of Pasteur's discoveries are shown by ♅, planet of originality, in the third. The ferocious energy with which he pushed his researches are amply accounted for by ♂ (energy) in third. ♂ is exalted in ♑. The fame they brought him is attributable to ☉ in ♑ in third; the money to ♀ in ♑ in third.

⊕ is in sixth. His material accumulations came almost wholly from his work in connection with health and disease (sixth). However, Pasteur remained poor by choice. ♂ ruling second △ ♃ in money sign, ♉, within 4° brought him a competence and might have brought him much more had he wished. He was, however, indifferent to money. ♇, co-ruler of second is close □ ♃. It has been pointed out that ♇ does everything exclusively. Indifference to money certainly renders one exclusive in that sense. It is not a general trait.

Pasteur lived long (to 73) as might be expected with so many planets in the long lived ♑. He might have lived much longer had he not so unmercifully driven himself all the days of his life. He died peacefully (♃ in eighth house). He was a devout Catholic to the last. (☽, part ruler of ninth, religion, in eighth, death). He was one of the most useful personages ever to live on this planet and all humanity owes him a debt of gratitude. He was born with a horoscope enabling him to perform the especial type of work which it was his life's mission to follow successfully. Had he known of astrology or believed in it he could have died knowing that he had utilized to the full the magnificent sidereal heritage with which he was endowed at birth.

CHAPTER XXI

Horoscopes of World Figures
(*Concluded*)

7.—A PLAYWRIGHT

8.—AN ARTIST

9.—AN INVENTOR

7.—GEORGE BERNARD SHAW
PLAYWRIGHT

THIS whimsical genius who has added so much to the gaiety of nations was born with ♊ rising and ☽ almost exactly on the ascending degree. ☉ is in ♌ and ☿, the ruler, in ♋. All three constitutions are therefore well represented.

As we might expect, Mr. Shaw has ☿ in the third house (writings). Everything he writes or has written since his youth up has found a ready market. It is not surprising therefore to find the ninth house (writings which are published) with ♑ on the cusp and ♄, ruler of ♑, in the second house (money). ♄ is ✳ ♇ in the money sign, ♉, and exact within 2°. ♃ squares ♄ closely and ♃ also rules published writings, but ♃ also is close ✳ ♀, money planet, and ✳ ☉ (5° orb). ☿ (writings) rules sign on cusp of money house, ♊, and is ✳ ♅ (5°) in the money sign, ♉. The native is wealthy and has a pronounced money sense, as we would expect, with ♄ in the second. ♄ also rules ♑, MidHeaven sign, and the native is equally canny in all affairs having to do with his profession. ♄ is in ♋ (detriment), which perhaps steered Mr. Shaw away from business and into the writing world as otherwise he has a very good business horoscope. Four planets and two angles cardinal give exceptional leadership ability, though the rising ♊ is not a leadership sign and ☽, also rising, is a bit uncertain on decisions. Mr. Shaw does presume to state his opinions in a very determined way as though he were the arbiter of the world's destinies. As, however, he does not have to follow them up with any particular action they are not likely to involve him in any serious difficulties, even when they turn out to be wrong—as they sometimes do.

The old gentleman is not nearly so set in his ways as he has contrived to make the world think. He has only two planets, neither of them of first importance, in fixed signs—and no fixed angles. At heart he is just feeling his way and hoping for the best like others who do not put up such an omniscient front. While undoubtedly a genius of sorts, Mr. Shaw has sold the world a bill of goods at a price possibly higher than the merchandise is really worth, as the natal chart fails to show the supernal wisdom of the ages which the native is so fond of impressing upon the world that he possesses. ☉ is essentially dignified in ♌, and ♆ in ♓. ♄, however, is in detriment in ♋, ♅ in fall in ♉, and ♇ in detriment in same sign. ♂ is also in its detriment in ♎. The native has almost worked miracles with a horoscope which, in spite of many aids to success, did not furnish him with the equipment usually found in the natal charts of those who climb high.

Yet Mr. Shaw writes very clever, entertaining plays. He exploits fields from which more orthodox writers would shy away in horror. Who but Shaw could make so grotesque a fantasy as "Pygmalion" acceptable, not merely to the highbrow but to the lowbrow public? The story is an impossible one but the playwright by his art gives it not merely possibility but probability—and more plausibility.

The hookup of the tenth, occupation, with the ninth, published writings, is obtained by ♑ appearing on the cusps of both houses and ♄, ruler common to both, in the money house. The unusual style of writing, so unique that a word—"Shavian"—has been coined to express it, is amply accounted for by ♅, exact △ the potent ♆, which not only is essentially dignified but is also the highest planet in the chart.

For all his native shrewdness, Shaw is a humanitarian at heart. His twelfth house contains 3 planets, ☊ and ⊕. He is much more "solitary" than would appear on the surface. A filled twelfth house gives a deep sense of retrospection and this one is reinforced by ♆ in ♓, twelfth house sign. Shaw must do a lot of pulling himself up by the roots to find out what makes him grow. Is Shaw as satisfied with Shaw as he claims to be? The generally benefic nature of the planets and aspects concerned with the twelfth indicates the answer to be yes, in the main. A couple of undersized flies in the ointment: ♃ □ ♄ and ♂, cuspal ruler, in detriment, may occasionally cause him to temper his self-satisfaction with a trifle of doubt, but on the whole Shaw highly approves of Shaw.

His lengthy tale of years is attributable to ♇, lethal ruler, ⚹ ♄ (2°). The latter planet bestows long life when hooked up favorably with death factors. ♃ rules ♐ on cusp of eighth (death) house, and its fine △ ♀ has already been commented on. This is another contributory factor. ♃'s □ ♄ is not so bad, as no benefic can wreak great harm, especially when other aspects counterbalance. ♊, however, is not an especially strong sign constitutionally and Shaw has taken excellent care of himself or, with ♂ and ☋ in sixth, he could hardly have contrived to go the long route of 84 years and still find himself in the excellent physical shape in which he is reported to be. He is helped by a strong ☉ in a strong sign, ♌.

His astonishing success in everything to do with the theatre (fifth house) is borne out by ☉ virtually exact ⚹ ☽. This "lucky" aspect has been a great protector to the native throughout his entire career.

The "lesson" of this chart to the student is that high success and world reputation may be wrested from a horoscope far from perfect in its endowments, by a soul great enough to make use of what it finds to hand without crying over what it lacks.

Bernard Shaw probably does not believe in Astrology. So far as we know nobody has had the temerity to ask him; though, as he has publicly stated he has no belief in an after life, he would hardly regard the Science of the Stars as worthy of his consideration. But Bernard Shaw is one of millions of living proofs of the truth of astrology. He exemplifies his horoscope in every conceivable way, but has done better with it than most of the millions of his fellow beings contrive to do with theirs.

8.—J. M. W. TURNER

FAMOUS ENGLISH LANDSCAPE PAINTER

The greatest of England's landscape artists, who won the praise of that most exacting of art critics, John Ruskin, came of the humblest beginnings. He was the son of a barber and strong attachment between him and his father existed to the latter's death. As would be expected ♎, art sign and ♀ art planet are very powerful. ♀ is essentially dignified in ♉ ♂ ♃ (5°) △ ♆, which gives magnificent creative imagination. The landscapes in which Turner excelled are indicated as his specialized type of work by ♄ (land) exalted in ♎ (art). ♑, an earthy sign, is rising and 4 of 9 planets are in earthy signs. (Note: Position of ♇ is not given owing to remoteness of the birth date). ♄ is highest planet in the chart. ⊕ shows source of the wealth. It is placed in ♎.

The curious impressionistic nature of Turner's paintings is the source of much of their charm. A sort of haze over his landscapes, unusual in the style of painting of his day, puzzled contemporary critics who, not seeing the countryside in that way, were at a loss to understand why Turner should. Many years after his death the theory was advanced that Turner was myopic and, his short sight not being corrected by glasses, that was the manner in which scenes appeared to him. The horoscope bears out the explanation. ☉ and ☽ jointly rule the eyes. A close affliction between the two will often indicate deficient vision when an important planet is in one of the so-called nebulous spots, afflicted by a malefic. One of these nebulae is in 28° ♉, termed the Pleiades.

In Turner's natal chart, his co-ruler, ♀, is in that exact degree, with ♂ in ♌ practically exact □. ☉ is also close □ ☽ (3°). ♀ is also afflicted by ♂ ♅ (3°). The myopic theory of Turner's style of painting is therefore in all probability the correct one.

This native could never learn to speak the English language correctly in spite of the cultural contacts he was able to make by the high esteem in which his work was held. ☿ (speech) ☌ ♄ (2°) demonstrates this incapacity. He lived to a great age (♑ rising— ♄ exalted in ♎ in eighth and △ ☽ within 1°) but his closing years were marred by some loss of his mental faculties. (Three planets in fourth—latter years—all afflicted by ♂; also ♅ afflicting ♀ and ♃ in fourth).

The second decan of ♑ which the native has rising bears this description: "If not too rash and headstrong native achieves great honors and rises to wide fame."

Turner was not too rash and headstrong.

9.—THOMAS A. EDISON

INVENTOR

Inventions and discoveries are ruled by ♅ and its sign, ♒. ♆ also takes a hand as it governs that which is secret, and inventors must tear from Nature her secrets by hard experimentation, study and thought.

Consequently we are not surprised to find that Edison has ☉, ☿ (mind planet) and ♆ all in ♒, and ♅

in ♈ which rules the brain. The redoubtable ♏ is rising. All 4 angles are fixed, 3 planets including ☉ and ☿ are fixed. ☽ is in the tenacious ♑, together with the ruler, ♂, who is exalted there. Four planets are cardinal but only 2 common. The native had a will of iron and a capacity for work which wore his assistants down to shadows. The horoscope is in every way outstanding and the native, like other great characters of history, has capitalized on every talent with which it provided him.

Still again we find the native's occupation indicated by an indirect significator. There is no planet in the MidHeaven. ♌ is on cusp, ruled by ☉, but ☉ is in the inventive ♒ ♂ ♆ (5°) ♂ ☿ (3°), and all are △ ♇ in 24° ♈, the △'s being very close. ♇'s exclusiveness is again in evidence. There was only one Edison. His methods and his business were utterly exclusive to himself. And ♇ is in the sixth house (service). It is, too, ♂ ♊ and it is Edison's ruler (♇ governs ♏ rising). It probably accounts for his deafness, though usually the twelfth house and ☿ are involved in this affliction. ♌ is in twelfth and Edison often termed his deafness a blessing with which he would not part, as it enabled him to concentrate without using up energy in shutting out the noises of a clamorous world.

The native never valued money, apart from the greater opportunities for service it provided. His indifference to it is shown by the two benefics square one another exact (♀ □ ♃). ♂, which in good aspect in the second and unafflicted gives enormous earning power, is ✳ ♀ (6°) ✳ ♄ (2°) ✳ ♆ (3°) ✳ ☉ (8°) △ ♇ (7°) ✳ Ascendant (4°). There are no afflictions. After that

nothing any other planet could do was of the least consequence in preventing Edison from becoming a millionaire—and never giving it a second thought.

Edison had advanced and very unorthodox religious
ideas, bordering on the occult (♌ in occult twelfth
house). His ⊕ is in the sixth sign, which in its larger
sense rules service to the race, and in the eleventh house
—hopes, wishes and ambitions. What he made materially from his work was all he ever could have hoped
for, but his real reward was in the transcendent service
he was able to render his fellow-men.

10. — NIKITA KHRUSHCHEV

USSR DICTATOR

One of the most outstanding features of the Russian
premier's natal chart is the impressive group of airy (mental) signs. Khrushchev is a deep thinker, a clever planner
and an ingenious maneuverer. He is seldom or never caught
napping and can outthink and outguess most of his opponents. His mind planet ☿ is the most elevated in the
horoscope. It is in the tenth house and Khrushchev's major
occupation is and has been since his peasant days—*thinking*.

The benefic ♌ conjoins his MidHeaven, which is ruled
by an unafflicted ♂ with a close △ to ♄ and a ✳ to ☿ .
The fierce nature of the personality is shown by a virtually
exact ♂ of ♂ and ☽ , both in the lethal eighth house. The
man has risen to power over the dead bodies of his enemies.
He himself has so far borne a charmed life, with both ☽
and ♂ among the best indicators in the chart.

But ♅ governs ♒ on the cusp of the eighth. It opposes
☉ and squares Ascendant. While subordinate to the

planet and luminary actually in the house, it must one day
have its inning. It is to be doubted if ♅, in spite of its
violent reputation when afflicted, will take precedence over
the two highly favorable significators in the house itself.
Also ♅ is in ♏, its exaltation sign, which tends to mitigate its adverse side.

The native's commanding position in the world is shown
by ☉ in the tenth but it will be noted that ☉ has two
afflictions and no good influences and this eminence can
hardly be considered as for the world's good. The eleventh
house — hopes, wishes and ambitions — contains three
planets with favorable aspects aggregating six and unfavorable four. But added to the favorable showing is ☿
ruling the intercepted ♊ — three to one favorable —
bringing the total to nine favoring and five adverse.

This does not tell the whole story, however. The tenth
house cuspal sign is ♉, and its ruler ♀ is exalted and
with no aspects of any kind, good or bad. This leaves ♀
entirely free to express its own benefic nature and gives
to the eleventh house an overwhelming preponderance of
good — for Khrushchev, if not for anyone else. Add to
all this the helpful influence of ♂ and ☽ in ♒, normal
eleventh house sign, and in spite of the bad ♅ the Aquarian ruler, the house is so enormously favorable that it completely accounts for the fantastic heights to which this
native has risen. He could hardly have held ambitions at
any time in his life for place and power higher than he
has achieved.

It is rather rare that a ruling planet is exalted and
with no aspects at all, and ♀ must be credited (or should
it be debited?) with aiding Khrushchev's climb from ob-
scurity to mightiness. He is having his troubles, of course,

but with twenty-one good aspects to thirteen bad ones (60% -40%) and with ♄ △ ☽ and △ ♂ , with Mid-Heaven ✳ ♆ ✳ ♇ ♂ ♌ , he is not likely to be unseated for a long time, if ever.

His remarkably good ♀ in the ninth house (dealings with other nations) seems to show that he really is anxious to keep the peace, which ♀ governs, in spite of his tough Martian talk. The possibility that he will be ousted eventually does not seem to be great. His fourth house (latter years of life) contains an exalted ♄ and is ruled by ♀ (♎ on the cusp). The one possibility is the afflicted ♅ , but this planet, also exalted, does not seem strong enough to overturn the favoring indicators.

If he does fall at last it is likely to be through bad judgment in old age — ♄ ☍ ☿ — but it does not seem that the world should bank on it. And his successor may not have an exalted, unaspected ♀ in the ninth house.

11. — LYNDON B. JOHNSON

VICE-PRESIDENT OF THE UNITED STATES

The tremendous drive and magnetic personality of this statesmanly figure is amply demonstrated by the striking aggregation of planets and luminaries in his first house.

With the ruling ♌ on the Ascendant, the ☉ is in ♂ with the rising degree and ☉, of course, governs ♌. Even in closer ♂ is the vigorous ♂, while ☿ the co-ruler and mind planet is also in the first (personality) house almost exact ♂ ☽. This last position denotes a very fine, clear mind, fully supported by the totally unafflicted ☿ with five good configurations.

The remarkable rise of this rugged individualist is astrologically accounted for by the almost perfect distribution of the planets by constitution — four cardinal, five fixed (including the angles), five common (including ⊙ and ☽). Leadership, determination, diplomacy, all are present in good measure. His life history shows that he has made utmost use of these talents. None has been buried in the earth.

Analysis of the elements, as is usually the case where the constitutions are well balanced shows a more uneven distribution. Fiery signs governing the intuitions and the religious sense are adequate, watery signs (emotion and feeling) reasonably so but, surprisingly, the airy group, representing the mentality, are scant, only ♇ and the Decendant appearing in this division. Anyone who sells Lyndon Johnson's mentality short on that account, however, will be making a serious mistake. His magnificent ☿ and a beautifully aspected ♇ in ☿ 's sign ♊ , and the most elevated planet in the chart, plainly demonstrates the high grade quality of the mind.

What is indicated by the lack of planets in the airy division is the wide diversification of the mental interests that many airy planets confer. Mr. Johnson is interested mentally in comparatively few things but his exceptional ☿ and five fixed signs demonstrate how one-pointedly he can concentrate on these interests. Politics have all along been his first love. He comes of a politically minded family and his early ambition was some day to be a United States Senator, a distinction he achieved at 40.

The tenth house is the house of Government, and ♇ , well aspected, the thing one can do better than most other people. Its position in this house speaks as clearly as if stated in language, of the achievements in this field of Lyndon Johnson.

The many planets in Virgo, the health sign, and its position in the first house (the body) have taken their toll. An appendicitis operation manifested the adverse influence of the ♂ -Ascendant ♂ . The 1955 heart attack the very close ♂ of ♂ with ☉ , ruling the heart. The Ascendant also governs this organ.

Johnson's horoscope shows 34 good aspects to 16 adverse — a ratio on the favoring side of more than two to one. From State Administrator for Texas of the National Youth Administration at 27 to Congressman at 28 to re-election at 32 to Naval Lieutenant Commander at 33 to U. S. Senator at 40 and Minority Leader at 44. Finally —or is it finally?—Vice-President at 52. Twenty-five years to reach the top—almost.

Will the "almost" be transcended? A meteoric career such as this certainly indicates the high favor of the astrological "gods," but Lyndon Johnson assuredly co-operated with his fine horoscope to the last possible influence. For the ultimate achievement, the Presidency, the ruler ☿ or ☉ up in the MidHeaven would almost set the seal of certainty on such a possibility and without such assistance it seems hazardous to indulge in flat forecasts. Saturn is badly afflicted and in fall and may forbid the highest office.

But with ♇ up there and so well aspected together with the powerful personality of the native himself, if he can stand the continuous strain of office without his health giving way, there might be a remote chance. ♇ , slowest moving planet in the Solar System and therefore of great power may outwit Saturn.

Johnson's grandfather announced to his neighbors the

birth of the future Vice-President with the words, "A United States Senator was born this morning—my grandson." The old gentleman fell short in his prophecy. A United States Vice-President was born that morning — a President... perhaps!

12.—NELSON ROCKEFELLER

GOVERNOR OF NEW YORK

A very acute summing up of the character of this distinguished political leader is in a biography which declares "Nelson Rockefeller is not a humble man." With ☉, five planets and all four angles in cardinal signs and only one in a common sign, his horoscope certainly says amen to that. The rather overdone term, "Born Leader" certainly fits him. In spite of the great things he has achieved, aided astrologically by seven of his ten planets up in the MidHeaven or close to it, the cardinal group is definitely too full. The ♎ Ascendant should be helpful in moderating what might otherwise be a somewhat arrogant personality.

Fixed signs contain ☽ and two planets, sufficient backing for the formidable cardinal division.

But the outstanding phenomenon of the chart to an informed astrologer must be the impressive ninth house. Rockefeller is known to be a deeply religious man; the breadth of his thinking, his munificent charities and his long range vision are here set forth in striking array. His role in organizing the United Nations was not a small one and his interest in developing the poorer areas of Latin America is well known. The ninth house, governing foreign affairs has bulked large in Nelson Rockefeller's life.

Yet in spite of a success that has been phenomenal his

horoscope in some respects is a difficult one. He is said by those who know him to be a complex character and with ☉, ♃, ♅ and ♆ all closely aspecting the Ascendant, this cannot be doubted.

His great inherited wealth is indicated by ♉ on the cusp of the eighth house, ruled by ♀ △ ☽ and ♂ ☉ ; also by ♃ △ ♄ . His ascent in the political world by ♃ in the tenth. It is astrologically recognized that ☉ ♂ MidHeaven, if reasonably well aspected tends to raise the native to high positions. In this chart not only ☉ but the ruler Venus is almost as elevated.

Interestingly enough ♇ is entirely without aspects and rules his second (money) house. ♇ is normally considered to be a malefic and there is no doubt that it rules death and general upsets. It is named (correctly) after ancient Pluto, god of the nether regions. Another god Pluto was, however, the deity that conferred immense wealth, hence our term "plutocracy." In very good aspect he is said to bestow more abundant riches than even ♃ but there is the condition that the native must be far ahead of average in intellect and vision. It would seem that Nelson Rockefeller would qualify.

Does the natal chart show presidential possibilities? Yes, undoubtedly, but that does not mean a certainty. In a contest the influences, natal and progressed, of each contestant have everything to do with the outcome. This was well illustrated in the National Presidential Election of 1960. Nixon's natal horoscope was slightly better than Kennedy's but the latter's progressed aspects were considerably better than Nixon's. To complicate the matter further, on the day of election Kennedy's aspects were terrible but Nixon's fairly good.

After three evenings of close study and the weighing of these decidedly conflicting influences the present author gave a close decision to Kennedy, based on his better progressions. Interviewed by the Press he stated that in his opinion Kennedy would "squeak through by the narrowest popular margin ever given a National President." The newspapers carried this, several days before the election and it proved to be so accurate that this again was carried as news.

Therefore unless and until Nelson Rockefeller decides to stand for President and until his opponent's birth time and progressions on election day are known, it would be hazardous to forecast that this ultimate prize would come to him.

But his horoscope, if it does not say yea, does not say nay.

CHAPTER XXII

And Finally—

I<small>T WILL</small> be evident to those who have studied this book that Vocational Astrology is no kindergarten subject to be picked up in a day. Simple in fundamentals, its ramifications are almost endless. Allowing wide latitude of choice, it nevertheless sternly bars certain vocations as obviously unfitted to a native; shakes its head doubtfully at others; bestows an indifferent glance on still another set, but beams all over in ecstatic approval when the right choices are finally reached.

These choices may be several. Even in the natal charts of the most successful there are usually indicators which if followed might have taken them to the top *via* an altogether different ladder than that which they actually elected to climb. There is, in fact, a school of thought (non-astrological) which holds that a really successful person in any line, no matter how specialized, could have been equally successful in anything else he had set his mind to. They except of course such vocations as call for special physical development. Astrologers are not likely to agree with them. If all the energy wasted in trying to teach music to children without a spark of musical talent had been used to analyze their horoscopes and arrive at what they were best fitted for, both the children and the neighbors would have benefited immeasurably.

Yet it would be a false conclusion to state that Edison

had to be an inventor, Shaw a playwright, Turner a painter or Hitler a dictator. There were other things these natives might have done and done well, still reaching heights of fame and affluence far above the crowd. True astrology will not hearken for a moment to the claptrap which so circumscribes the fate that a man is born to be and do this, that or the other and nothing besides. Perhaps the very greatest figures who so influence the destiny of the world that had they not been born all events would have been changed, do have their ordained work mapped out for them. But where shall we draw the line? If Edison had not lived these words might be penned by the light of an oil lamp instead of by electric light. Or they might not—perhaps someone else would have found a suitable filament by now.

On the other hand, the world might not have been so very different a place had George Bernard Shaw not honored it with his presence. It probably would be a much more comfortable place had Mr. Hitler succeeded in getting the art education he wanted and left political agitation alone.

Who shall say? These speculations take us into the realm of advanced metaphysics and really have no place in this work except as a partial answer to the fallacy, "I'm bound to be what the horoscope says I shall be." We earnestly hope no student will approach the subject from that hopeless angle, otherwise this book has been written in vain. We *must* act on the theory that we have freewill, and this implies freedom of choice of a vocation. The ineffectual leaning back and waiting for fate to do something for one, so characteristic of an excess of common signs, has ruined many promising careers.

Some modern Hogarth might well limn the wretched down-and-outers parading up and down the "Market Streets" of any large city and give this picture the title, "They Waited for Something to Happen." Something always does happen, of course, to those who wait long enough. Everyone has an eighth house.

The student is urged to take the vocational indicators in the horoscope seriously and it is believed that he will never find them to let him down. A vast specialized field exists for vocational guidance by astrology, and a field of the greatest helpfulness. It is not too early for parents to have a child's horoscope examined by an expert in this work immediately after birth—at least before he starts to school—so that his training may proceed along lines exactly in harmony with what the horoscope shows as his natural vocational bent.

There are no "hopeless" horoscopes. Even in the natal charts of those who are pointed to as overtowering successes in their particular professions, there are often afflicted malefics, weak benefics, squares, oppositions and detriments. Always there is ☲ somewhere, to put his blight on whatever he touches. Yet elsewhere in the world are those with charts approximately the same, who have made only mediocre successes where their astrological counterparts are up in the top brackets. And there is no one, however exalted, who could not in some way have done better, had he been guided by the indicators of his natal chart.

It is unfortunate that one has to point to a character like Hitler for evidence of the truth of this assertion. He is, however, the one outstanding world figure known to use astrology in every important decision he makes.

The general staffs of Britain and our own country are copying and trying to improve upon Hitler's own novel military methods. There is, therefore, nothing out-of-the-way in suggesting that his astrological methods might be followed by all with equally effective results. The rain of heaven falls alike upon both just and unjust, as do the influences of the heavens. Why permit only the unjust to apply them and secure the benefit of knowing how they work?

The true student of Astrology is always a student. He may obtain his "instructor's rating," may set up in professional practice and even have his astrological conclusions reported by the Associated Press. Regardless of this, he continues to learn while he teaches. No day goes by that he does not add something to his store of astrological knowledge. Everyone he meets is an experimental subject. He notes here a ♌ trait, there a quirk of ♐, a touch of typical ♈ dominance, the quiet humor of a ♎ or the wisecrack of a ♊. He may have no idea of the date or time of birth of any of them, but by their ways he knows them. Life is never dull for the astrologer so long as he has people to watch. And if there is none around he can go back to his own self-examination, which perhaps teaches him even more.

One day, at long last, the ancient and honorable science of Astrology shall be restored once more to the position of dignity and respect it occupied in the remote past. Emperors and Kings, Statesmen and Popes were glad to make it their study and to encourage its exponents. Then came the charlatans who turned it into a racket, and it fell in the social and intellectual scale until, a couple of generations ago, none was so poor to do it reverence. The efforts of such great astrologers as Leo, Sepharial and others who devoted their lives to study and research gradually started to tilt the balance in the other direction, until, today, there is a recrudescence of interest among the educated very heartening to those who love and believe in the science and work for its restoration to intellectual favor.

Meantime the public continues to buy the astrological lucubrations to be found in the Ten Cent Stores, and to deposit pennies in weighing machines for a card giving not only the weight but the horoscope. Perhaps this kind of "astrology" will always be with us, but it adds immeasurably to the task of those who labor for a restored science of the stars to have to overcome the prejudices roused in the thinking by these popular fallacies.

In the final analysis, only by his own hard study and experiment, constant watching of results, and associating them with their appropriate natal influences, can the student arrive at the absolute certainty of the truth of Astrology which never again can be shaken. That is indeed a happy outcome for it furnishes him with a sure guide for the remainder of his life which will, if he follows it sincerely, never fail him. Whether he will acquire this certainty to the full, depends largely upon what kind of a fourth house he possesses—the house of "outcomes."

Here's hoping he has a good one.

Meaning of the Symbols Used

SIGNS

Aries	♈
Taurus	♉
Gemini	♊
Cancer	⊗
Leo	♌
Virgo	♍
Libra	♎
Scorpio	♏
Sagittarius	♐
Capricorn	♑
Aquarius	♒
Pisces	♓

PLANETS

Sun	☉
Moon	☽
Mercury	☿
Venus	♀
Mars	♂
Jupiter	♃
Saturn	♄
Uranus	♅
Neptune	♆
Pluto	♇

OTHER SYMBOLS

Dragon's Head (Moon's North Node)   ♌

Dragon's Tail (Moon's South Node)   ☋

Part of Fortune   ⊕

MidHeaven   M.C. or MC

ASPECTS

Sextile	(60°)	Favorable	✳
Trine	(120°)	Very Favorable	△
Square	(90°)	Unfavorable	□
Opposition	(180°)	Very Unfavorable	☍

POSITIONS

Conjunction	(0°)	☌
Parallel	(0° of Declination)	P

Some Explanations

(1) Throughout this work, as in most astrological books and delineations, ☉ and ☽ are referred to as planets, which of course they are not. The correct term for either of these bodies is "luminary" or "light."

It is inconvenient and cumbersome, however, when considering ☉ and ☽ together with the planets to keep differentiating them by use of the above terminology. The practice has therefore developed of including ☉ and ☽ under the generic term "planets" together with the rest.

(2) ♂'s and P's are not "Aspects" but "Positions." They are loosely referred to sometimes as aspects for the same reason that ☉ and ☽ are often referred to as "planets."

(3) Figures in parentheses occurring after the listing of an aspect or position indicate how far from exact such aspect or position is.

Thus ☉△☽ (5°) or (5) shows that this trine is within 5° of exactness. "Within orb" of 5° is the technical term.*

* "The Unit System of Judging Planetary Influences," by Charles E. Luntz (David McKay Publishing Co., Philadelphia: 50 cents), is a standard reference work dealing with the strength of the various aspects, positions, exaltations, etc.

Planetary Index of Occupations

A

Accessory Makers, Toilet ♀
Accountants ☿
Acoustic Experts ☿
Actors ♀
Actuaries ☿
Advertising Agents ♃
Ad-Writers ♃
Airplane Mechanics ♅
Aldermen ♃
Amusement
 Concessionaires ♀
Anaesthetists ♆
Appraisers ♃
Architects ☿

Armament Makers and
 Workers ♂
Army Officers ♂
Artists ♀
Art Museum Curators ♀
Assayers ♂
Astrologers ♅, ♆
Authors ☿
Automobile Manufacturers
 and Dealers ♅
Automobile Mechanics ♅
Automobile Racers ♅
Aviators ♅

B

Bakers ☽
Bankers ☉
Bank Tellers ☉
Barbers ♂
Bath House Proprietors ☽
Beach Life Guards ♆
Beauty Parlor Operators ♀
Bee Keepers ☿, ♀
Boat Owners ☽
Bond Salesmen ♃

Bookbinders ☿
Bookkeepers ☿
Boxers ♂
Brewers ☽
Brewery Workers ☽
Bricklayers ♄
Builders ♄
Bus Drivers ☿
Butchers ♂
Buyers ☿

C

Cabbage and Cauliflower
 Growers ☽

Candy Manufacturers ♀
Cap and Hat Makers ♂, ♀

G

Garage Proprietors ♅
Gardners ♄
Gin Manufacturers ☉
Glassware and Chinaware
  Manufacturers ☽
Gold, Workers in ☉
Governesses ☿

Grain Dealers ♄
Grocers, Retail ☿
Grocers, Wholesale ♃
Guards ♂
Guides ♃
Gun Makers ♂

H

Hairdressers ♂, ♀
Handwriting Experts ☿
Hardware Manufacturers
  and Dealers ♂
Hat and Cap Makers ♂, ♀
Healers ☿
Healers, Faith ♅
Heart Specialists ☉

Hides, Dealers in ♄
Horse Trainers ♃
Hotel Keepers and
  Workers ♀
Household Help (Female) ☽
House Painters and
  Paperhangers ♀

I

Illustrators ♀
Implement Makers ♂
Impresarios ☉
Information Clerks ☿
Instructors ☿
Instrument Manufacturers
  and Dealers ♅

Interior Decorators ♀
Interpreters ☿
Inventors ♅
Investment Bankers ☉
Iron and Steel Workers ♂

J

Jewelers ☉
Jockeys ♃

Judges ♃
Jugglers ☿

L

Laborers ♄
Landscape Gardeners ♀

Laundry Proprietors and
  Workers ☽

Lawyers ♃
Leather Goods Manufacturers and Dealers ♄
Lecturers ☿, ♅
Life Insurance Salesmen ♇

Lighting Specialists ♅
Liquor Dealers ☽
Locksmiths ♂
Lumberjacks ♂

M

Machinists ♂
Maids ♀
Mail Carriers ☿
Mechanics ♂
Medical Men ☿
Melon Growers ☽
Merchandise Managers ☿
Messengers ☿
Metal Workers ♂
Metaphysicians ♅
Midwives ☽

Milkmen ☽
Milliners ♀
Mind Readers ♆
Miners ♄
Money Lenders ♀
Monks ♄
Motormen ♅
Movie Theatre Owners ♅
Moving Picture Producers ♅
Mushroom Growers ☽
Musicians ♀, ♆

N

Naval Officers ♆
Nerve Specialists ☿, ♅
Night Watchmen ♄
Night Workers ♄

Notaries Public ☿
Nuns ♄
Nurses ☽

O

Obstetricians ☽
Occultists ♅
Occult Writers ♆
Office Help ☿

Oil Well Operators ♆
Oil Workers ♆
Orange Growers ☉
Orators ☿

P

Painters, House ♀
Paperhangers ♀
Paper Manufacturers ☿
Park Keepers ☉
Peach Growers ♀

Perfume Manufacturers ♀
Pharmacists ♆
Photographers ♀
Physicians ☿
Plastic Artists ☽

Playground Directors ☉

Plumbers ♄

Poets ♆

Policemen ♂

Politicians ☉

Poultry Raisers ☽

Priests ♄

Printers ☿

Prison Guards ♆, ♂

Private Investigators ♆

Psychotherapists ♅

Publications, Writers for ♃

Publishers ☿, ♃

Pugilists ♂

Pursers ♀, ♃

R

Racing Stable Owners and Workers ♃

Radio Announcers ☿, ♅

Radio Manufacturers and Dealers ♅

Real Estate, Dealers in ♄

Recorders of Deeds ☿

Reporters ☿

Research Workers ♅

Restaurant Proprietors and Workers ☽

Retail Grocers ☿

S

Sailors ☽

Salesmen ☿

Scientists ♅

Secretaries ☿

Sextons ♄

Shoe Manufacturers and Dealers ♃

Shoe Workers ♃

Singers ♀

Social Secretaries ♀

Social Service Workers ♅

Society Editors ♀

Soldiers ♂

Speakers ☿

Sporting Goods Manufacturers and Dealers ♃

Spotlight Operators ☉

Stationers ☿

Stenographers ☿

Stock Exchange Workers ☉

Stock Raisers ♂

Stock Speculators ☉

Storekeepers ☿

Street-car Conductors ☿

Surgeons ♂

T

Tailors ♀

Tanners ♄

Tavern and Taproom Owners and Helpers ☽

Teachers ☿

Telegraphers ♅

Telephone Operators ☿, ♅

Tellers ♀

Theatre Owners and
  Managers ☉

Throat Specialists ♀

Time Keepers ♄

Tombstone Makers ♄

Train Conductors ☿

Travelling Men ☽

Treasurers ♀

Trial Lawyers ♀, ♃

Typists ☿

U

Underground Workers ♄

Undertakers ♄, ♇

V

Vocational Specialists ☿, ♄

W

Waiters and Waitresses ☽

Walnut Growers ☉

Wardens ♆

Watchmen ☽

Whale Hunters ♃

Wholesale Grocers ♃

Women's Apparel Manufac-
  turers and Dealers ♀

Woolen Merchants ♃

Wrestlers ♂

Writers ☿

X

X-Ray Workers ♅

PLUTO (♇)

(With some notes on ♆ and ♅)

A great deal has been learned about the vocational influence of this planet during the past twenty years. Reasoning by analogy and then observing how closely the facts conformed to the reasoning has led to the conclusions expressed in this chapter.

Thus it was established soon after ♇ was discovered that it undoubtedly governed physical death, that it did, in fact, take precedence over ♂ , which had never been regarded as quite answering the question of planetary death rulership. It was also quickly recognized that ♇ ruled modern dictators, totalitarian governments, all-out war (not small wars or the individual combats world wars include, which are in the domain of ♂). Other unhappy products of the present age—organized crime, gangsterism, even the wholesale juvenile delinquency that has flourished since 1930 when ♇ 's existence was first verified —trace to this planet's influence.

It is well known that the discovery of a "new" planet (new to the world but not to the universe) marks a decided quickening of everything the planet influences. ♅ , discovered in 1781, definitely marked the beginning of the industrial age. It was in 1781 that James Watt obtained his patent covering a device for driving machinery by steam power. There had been crude mechanical contrivances prior to that but the birth from this tiny but important beginning of modern industry took place in the year ♅ appeared on the scene. Reference to the occupations listed under ♅ in Chapter III will show that almost all of them were unknown prior to the planet's discovery.

Even the esoteric rulerships of ♅ have brought modernization in these fields. Thus Astrologers, Occultists, Faith Healers and Clairvoyants come in part under the dominance of ♅ and in part under ♆. Certainly these occupations have been with the race since earliest times, but they have been pursued scientifically and with the research system of modern technique only since ♅ revealed himself. Discovery of ♆ sixty-five years later enhanced these precise methods still further.

In 1846 August Leverrier announced the discovery of ♆ which rules oil as applied to industrial use. (Oil for lighting is governed by ☽). Eleven years later the first oil wells were sunk in Rumania and two years after that in the United States. Interestingly enough it was irregularity in the motion of ♅ that led to the discovery of ♆, almost as though the former was trying to give a clue to the fact that the latter existed. While this may only be a poetic fancy, it is an astrological fact that the two planets are co-rulers of a number of the same things and seem to have influences largely in common with each other.

The facts regarding ♅ and ♆ are cited as supporting analogous facts respecting ♇. Analogies are useful in constructing theories, but theory is not fact, and facts must never be distorted to make them conform to theories that have been built around them. But if, as is now known, ♇ rules death and the monstrous things recorded above when in adverse aspect or without aspects, then the favorable things he governs must bear some relationship in an opposite way to the unfavorable. This is always the case with the Sun, Moon and planets. Their bad side invariably is contrastingly opposite to their good side.

To demonstrate this by a few examples: ⊙ well aspected indicates dignity; badly aspected, boastfulness. ♃ alone or in favorable aspect, abundance of good; unfavorable, abundance of trouble. ♄ well influenced, thrift; alone or badly influenced, miserliness. ♅ with good configurations, originality; alone or badly configurated, eccentricity.

The rulerships of ♇ alone or badly aspected can be summed up in two words, THE EXCLUSIVE. Death is certainly the most exclusive thing that can happen to an individual and it can occur only once in a lifetime. A dictator has to be exclusive. There can be only one of him or he is no longer sole dictator. Organized crime usually traces to one "big shot" who dominates the organization. Juvenile delinquency, of the vicious kind almost unknown in former years, seems to be an exclusive product of the present generation.

So if ♇ afflicted or by its own malefic self rules the harmful exclusive, surely ♇ well favored by the aspects must govern the helpful exclusive. Observation ranging over a period of 30 years, shows that it does. This was suspected even 20 years ago when the first edition of this book appeared. The statement made then in listing ♇'s occupational rulership was this:

"It is hazardous at present to use ♇ as a significator of occupation." That statement has been allowed to stand in the present edition, but with a supplementary footnote.

Even then the listing gave as one of ♇'s rulerships "The Entirely Exclusive." It can now be enlarged to read "Things one can do better than most others in his circle." This gives us an important new vocational element for exploration. The traditional rules as set forth in this book will certainly not be affected but a new factor is introduced to augment them. This can only be employed, however, if ♇ has more and stronger good aspects than adverse, and if it is in some way connected beneficently with the MidHeaven, tenth house, ♑ , ♄ or one of the vocational indicators. Otherwise it is of no occupational value.

What this means in practice (assuming it can be used) is that the native has some exceptional talent in a certain direction that should be utilized in the occupation, whatever it is. The function of a helpful ♇ is to pinpoint a particular adroitness that considerably exceeds the prevailing average and that can bring the native into special prominence by his unusual ability in this direction.

The special faculty need not be original—that is the function of ♅ . It may be some ability that has been known since the dawn of time. It is exclusive not as against all the world (although that occasionally happens as in the case of Edison and Ford) but as contrasted with the abilities of others in the limited circle of the native's associates or of the professional or industrial group with which he is affiliated.

The nature of the special skill may be determined by the following house positions of ♇ :

1st All-around efficiency.

2nd Exceptional money sense.

3rd Unusual skill in expression of ideas.

4th Very shrewd real estate appraisal ability.

5th Investment sagacity.

6th Keen judge of human nature.

7th Diplomatic skill.

8th (Pluto's own house) Able executor.

9th Impressive far-sightedness.

10th Unique business or professional talent.

11th Remarkable capacity for making friends.

12th Unwonted breadth of outlook.

All of these special and unique powers are *adaptable* to the occupation but do not *indicate* the occupation. They are usable whatever this may be and if ♇ is good enough to rely on in these respects, great thought should be given as to how they best may be applied.

It should first be ascertained, however, that ♇ has sufficient strength on the favorable side to make its help possible. Reliance on an adverse or indifferent ♇ can only bring disappointment. In such a case forget him (or her, as ♇ is a feminine planet) and trust to your really good planets aided by your own constructive thought and intelligent action to bring you such success as your horoscope shows is possible for you.

Which is usually far greater than those astrologically uninformed would regard as attainable.

INDEX